Flashir

GW01418593

Kelly Brown

Copyright © 2024 Kelly Brown

ISBN: 978-1-917425-16-2

All rights reserved, including the right to reproduce this book, or portions thereof in any form. No part of this text may be reproduced, transmitted, downloaded, decompiled, reverse engineered, or stored, in any form or introduced into any information storage and retrieval system, in any form or by any means, whether electronic or mechanical without the express written permission of the author.

Foreword

I really didn't know what I was letting myself in for when I met Kelly for coffee in November 2023. I assumed we'd have a good natter and put the world as we saw it to rights. I was aware of the tragedy Kelly had gone through in losing Mero, and as a woman and mother I felt for her pain. Knife crime, I assumed was something that happened to 'those people' 'over there'. I had brought my children up well, so thought they were exempt from that world. But after helping Kelly write her story, I now realise it can happen to anyone, anywhere. Special K has taken her heartbreak, grief and despair and has channelled it positively by writing about her experiences, raising knife crime awareness, installing bleed cabinets, setting up the Mero's World Foundation, and the Youth Hub, and finally not to mention helping to educate and change the mindset of the next generation to the devastating, and life-changing consequences that making the decision to carry a knife will bring, not only to the victim's family, but also to their own loved ones.

Jennifer Silcott, Writer

Dedications

Kelly was brave enough to let me interview her for the knife crime documentary '*No Safe Place*' only a few short months after Mero's tragic death. It was the hardest thing I've ever had to do. Kelly, you are an inspiration to so many.
Jacqui Carroll, Director REELMCR

I first met Kelly in the weeks following Rhamero's death. Despite the terrible grief, it was clear she was already resolved to do everything she could to stop these terrible events from happening to another family.
Afzal Khan MP

I am proud of Kelly. It's taken heart and courage to write her book. It's an honest and raw story of a woman who lost her child but gained a new outlook on life.
Matthew Norford, Chair of 1 Message

This book gives you a full picture of the sad tragedy Kelly faced when losing her baby boy, which really is every parent's worst nightmare. Refusing defeat, she uses every ounce of her energy to ensure no other parent has to deal with losing a child to knife crime. Kelly, you are a true testament of strength, courage, but most of all, a MOTHER'S LOVE. I know Mero is so proud of you.
Love, Naomi x

The latest figures for Greater Manchester suggest proactive policing and preventative work is delivering real results. In the twelve months to August 2023, GMP recorded 3,732 knife crimes, which is 668 fewer than the previous year – a reduction of 15.2 per cent.

Wider serious violent offences, which includes robbery and violence and violence with injury, was down to 35,397.

Roy Thickett

Chapter One
Who was Mero? Where do I begin....?

Mero was a loving baby, and he had so much character about him, cheeky but in a cute kind of way. He was always falling and banging his head in his early years. Errol and I were worried at one point, and we were going to get him a helmet to protect his head when he rode his scooter and bicycle. I can even remember getting a call from the school when Mero was in reception. I was told he was okay, but we needed to collect him because of the lump on his head. I only lived five minutes from the school, and when I picked him up, he was happy within himself, but the size of the lump on his head was huge. Errol and I were concerned and took him to the hospital, but we were told by the doctor that there was nothing to worry about, because the lump came out straight away.

Mero was one baby who stole the hearts of many friends and family, especially his nana Eldora, who would buy him his favourite foods and cook him chicken and dumplings. I think this had a lot to do with the fact he looked like Errol, as well as his cheeky and loving personality. When Mero was about three years old, we had a routine where we would put him to bed and close the baby gate at the top of the stairs. One evening, Errol and I were watching TV, and the living room door suddenly opened, and Mero appeared. We laughed and asked him how he managed to get downstairs. He showed us how he climbed over the baby gate, holding on to the banister and walking down the stairs. This was one of the reasons Errol called him a monkey, because as he was growing up, he was always climbing.

Mero was a little joker, always joking around no matter where he was. His favourite thing was to play around in the house, to hide and then jump out and scare me when I got in from work, or when I came out of the shower. He also had the most annoying habit of wiping his armpits and smearing it across your face, and saying, 'Smell that'. Mero was the son I could have a laugh with, always about anything, whereas Remi was the serious one. I liked to take selfies and out of nowhere Mero seemed to pop up in the background of the picture. He also liked to put his feet on you and then laugh with his infectious laugh, which you could hear before you saw him. When he played on his computer, or was on the phone in his room, he was very loud, and we'd have to shout up and tell him to keep the noise down. Mero loved music and playing on his PS4, mainly at night, and on rainy days he would stay in playing games with a bag of sweets next to him. He loved strawberry flavoured Chewits, Dairy Milk and always a fizzy drink, and if I wasn't cooking, he'd ride up to a chicken shop on Lloyd Street called Dallas and buy some chicken wings and chips.

He was a sporty boy, and from the age of six he played football for the Fletcher Moss Rangers, being one of the fastest in his team. Mero was in Year Four and in the school's sports day, he was taking part in the cross country run around Platt Fields Park. All the children were lined up, the teacher blew the whistle, and they all set off running at a steady pace, and I noticed Mero started running ahead of the other children, and I was screaming and shouting encouragement. When he was on the second lap, all the other parents were shouting for him too. He was starting to get tired, and his friends ran alongside him to keep his spirits up. Everyone was shouting his name, and I felt overwhelmed with the love shown to my son. As he crossed the finish line, Mero fell into his dad's arms, who was waiting for him, and he finished the race well ahead of the other children.

Mero was a messy boy. His bedroom and whichever room he went into was always a mess. Growing up, he wasn't really bothered about clothes and his appearance until he started high school. Then he wanted designer clothes, mainly North Face, and he did chores around the house so he could save for the things he wanted. He was a boy who took pride in his personal appearance. If his hair wasn't in plaits, he would always have it out and wet, and so wet his curls would be dripping with water all over the house, and I would shout at him to go and dry his hair. Mero had the most beautiful skin complexion. He had long dark, curly hair and small brown eyes, and when he spoke it was with a lisp. He was a normal moody teenager, but which teenager isn't? If he didn't get his own way, or wasn't allowed out, my glass doors in the living room would get slammed shut and he would stomp upstairs, all the while mumbling under his breath. His favourite phrase when he didn't get his own way was: 'You're snide'. So, there were many days he would sneak out of the house to meet his mates.

One year I went to see my cousin who lived in Rhyl, with my sister and her kids and Mero. It was a hot day, and we were sitting in the garden, but the kids wanted to go to the beach, so we let them go because they were sensible. After about an hour they all came back, covered in black stuff from the waist down, which had a fishy odour, and we asked them what it was, and Mero replied that it was fish poo. When they were coming back, they came the wrong way and walked in fish poo or sewage on the beach. We all started laughing. They were sinking in the stuff and Mero started crying, thinking that he was going to get stuck. My cousin Stuart had to hose them down before he let them go into the house to have a shower.

Mero loved organising sleepovers with his cousins, where there was so much noise and banter between them. He would organise singing competitions with his Uncle Duane, who he would ask to stay each Christmas, and it was nice to hear them giggling all through the night. Most weekends he was never at home, every chance he got he'd stay at my sister's house. She was like a second mum to him, and they got on well.

There was a seven-year age gap between Remi and Mero. They had their differences but most of the time they got on, and even more so when Errol and I split. It was like Remi stepped in and acted as a father figure to Mero. Mero and his dad did have a good relationship. Mero was his boy, but when he left, he became distant with the boys and there was a period where there was no contact between them. Mero struggled with this distance and could not forgive his dad, and their relationship never recovered.

Unfortunately, Mero went down a rocky path, and one day I'm not joking fifteen officers came to my house. I was in the living room bathing my grandson

Caerus with Remi and Errol. Mero was upstairs in his room, and then I heard shouting and saw officers in my garden. They came in through the back door, and as Mero came downstairs, they hand-cuffed him. I asked them why they were taking Mero, and they replied that Mero and his friends had taken a bike from someone. So, I said, 'It takes this many officers to arrest my son, does it?' They didn't and couldn't answer me, and then they took Mero to the station. Errol went with him, and after a few hours they charged him with theft and then released him.

Mero loved music and thought he might get into modelling one day. He also wanted to go to college. He wanted to be normal and to be with his mates and get into a routine, because he felt isolated at being home schooled from the age of fourteen. He was a very popular boy and had different friendship groups at school and from Fallowfield. In primary school he was very bright and achieved good grades. He was popular not only with other kids, but with the teachers too. He had a heart of gold; if he saw someone with shopping bags, he would offer to carry them. He was very polite and respectful to the older generation. He chose to do catering at college, because from time to time he liked cooking at home.

The last picture I have of Mero is of when he went to London to be A J Tracey's younger self in a music shoot. He was picked out of 250 boys to do this part. At first, I wasn't going to let him go, because he was only sixteen, but I had a chat with Errol, and the guy who was taking Mero to London, and we decided to let him go. He was doing something I knew it meant a lot to him. Prior to this, I bought Mero an Armani tracksuit for his upcoming birthday, and he asked if he could wear it, because he wanted to look good for the music shoot. The morning of 8 of September, Mero went off to London, keeping in regular contact with me throughout the day. He sent me a picture of him standing outside the shoot next to a very flashy car. He told me he'd met A J Tracey, but the shoot didn't end up happening because A J wasn't happy with the set. Mero said that he was happy because he got three hundred pounds and a bag full of goodies for doing it. I'm glad I let Mero go because that was the last picture taken of him.

I miss him calling me Kelly instead of mum to wind me up, and the way he would say 'I love you'. I miss him riding to my workplace to ask for money for a takeaway, especially if I wasn't going to cook. I miss the loud yawn coming from his bedroom every morning. There are so many memories I now hold in my heart. My house has gone from a house full of laughter, noise and warmth, to a house that is so quiet, you can hear a pin drop. Mero was the heart and soul of the family. Without his presence, the emptiness that has been created saddens me. Mero was my second heartbeat, Remi being my first, but loving them the same. My heart almost stopped beating the day Mero took his last breath. My baby boy will forever be in my heart, and he is deeply missed.

'You will always be my baby boy.'

Chapter Two

I was staying at my sister, Naomi's house because of two occasions where a group of boys had come to my family home. The first incident was around eight weeks before Mero's death. Remi, Mero, and I were all upstairs in our bedrooms. It was about ten o'clock in the evening. I was asleep and then at about eleven o'clock, Remi came into my room and asked if I had heard anything. I replied that I hadn't, as once I was asleep, I wasn't woken easily. Mero came out of his room, and we heard a car screech off. I then checked my exterior camera. A car had pulled up, full of boys, and I could hear one boy say, 'It's that house there, with the light on.' (We always leave the hall light on). Then I heard, 'Mero, I'm going to slap it at your gaff,', which is slang for 'shooting at the house'. I phoned the police and showed them the footage, telling them what had happened. They logged it and I was told they would send someone out in the morning. I was worried and couldn't really sleep, and I messaged Errol to let him know what had happened.

The next morning, a police officer came to my house, and I showed him the footage on my phone, and I was told there was nothing they could do because he couldn't see the registration plate, or the colour of the car. He gave me a crime reference number and off he went. The next day, Errol and my sister came round. She said it wasn't safe for me to stay there. Remi stayed at home, while Mero and I went to stay with my sister, who was living in a townhouse in town. I had two weeks of going to work and coming back to my sister's house, which was tough because I had a house of my own, but we had to live out of one bedroom because I was scared, I didn't feel safe, and I worried for Mero's safety.

I asked Mero who the boys were, and he replied that he didn't know. In the end I couldn't take it any longer and went back to my house, and Mero continued to stay with Naomi. I felt relieved to be back at home in my own environment, surrounded by my belongings. Around the end of July, before I was going to break up from work, I was at home chilling. Remi came in and said he was going to stay at Sadie's, his girlfriend's house. Once he had gone, I went upstairs to have a bath, and get ready for bed, and then watched television for a while. At around ten o'clock, I turned off the television, and went to sleep, keeping the hall light on. Then around five o'clock in the morning I was woken up by a loud crashing noise. I jumped out of bed and ran to the hall, and through the hallway window I saw a car speeding off. I ran downstairs to find the kitchen windows and the windows of Remi's car, which was parked on the drive, smashed. I phoned Remi and Errol and Naomi and told them what had happened. I was shaking and could just about speak on the phone.

I then phoned the police, and while I was waiting for them to arrive, Errol and Naomi came. We didn't touch anything until the police came, and they finally arrived around midday. My sister kept saying it wasn't safe for me to stay at home. Three police officers came into the house from the back doors and looked at the bricks and the broken windows, and then gave me a crime reference. They didn't take any pictures, or ask me if I was okay, nothing. It was as if they weren't bothered in the slightest. When Remi came home, he was upset that I had been home alone when it had happened. Once Errol had gone, we cleaned up the glass and I took pictures of the damage.

As soon as it got to nine o'clock, I phoned the housing and told them what had happened. They asked me if I had contacted the police and had a crime reference number, and I replied that I had. I was then told that someone would come out to board up my windows, so I waited with Naomi. We cleaned the glass from the front garden and one of my neighbours gave us a car cover for Remi's car on the driveway. The maintenance man didn't come until eight o'clock that evening, and once the windows were boarded up, I packed my things and went back to my sister's house. The summer holidays had started, and I was off work, and I was sitting in my room thinking that I was a grown woman; I should be at home, not at my sister's house. But it wasn't safe for me or the boys to go back there. I got in touch with the housing and asked if they could put my name forward to move. I was told this couldn't happen because of my rent arrears, but this didn't deter me, and I looked for other ways to move. I looked for house exchanges on every site possible. I even got in touch with my local councillor, Jade Doswell, and told her my situation, and she tried her best to see what she could do to help. It was hard not being able to move, and I felt helpless as a mum, wanting to protect my children.

I spent the holidays in the house, not wanting to see anybody. I was constantly emailing Jade and the housing to see if anything had changed regarding my circumstances, but still nothing. Most of the time I felt like I was invading my sister's space and privacy, and I struggled, but being the type of person I am, I kept it all in and tried my best to find a solution. I felt angry and disappointed that when I asked for help from the police and the housing, I didn't receive any. No one was listening to me and taking the threats to my home seriously. I couldn't go back home because it clearly wasn't safe. What really got to me was the police and the housing only wanted to help after Mero was killed, and not before. Where were their safeguarding policies for my son, for me, and for Remi? One Manchester Housing cleared my arrears and placed me in the top housing band for a move after being informed of Mero's death.

I was searching every day for a house in a suitable area, knowing I didn't want to rush things. It had to be right, and at the same time I was disgusted that it had to come to this. I was moving with only one child; Mero should have been moving with us. As for Greater Manchester Police, and the officers involved, I spoke to Tracey about my concerns and she lodged a complaint with the Independent Office for Police Conduct, concerning how the officers dealt with me on the two occasions they'd visited my house. I first met Chantel Miller, who was the lead investigator, and Sophie Mellor, the case supervisor, in one of the meeting rooms upstairs at Longsight Library. I was with Claire Simister, a police officer who was supporting me. Chantel was there to investigate my complaints. We introduced ourselves and then she asked me to explain what had happened in the run up to Mero being killed. Chantel made me feel comfortable and made me aware that it would be a long process, but she was going to do what she could. The investigation is on-going, and I receive regular emails from Chantel keeping me up to date with the progress of my complaint.

Following on from this, I had a meeting with two officers from the Manchester City Council Safeguarding Team. They were putting together a new document regarding Mero's death. The meeting was held in a quiet room in the town hall, where I was asked to share my story on the run up to Mero being killed. At one point, I broke down and cried and was given a tissue to wipe my tears. I was asked if I was okay to continue, and I replied that I was. They wrote down all the information I gave, and they asked if they could use it. I gave my permission, clearly stressed and unhappy that this situation should never have happened, and in the new document they were writing, Mero was to be their Child A. I wanted answers and I was hitting out at everyone who had failed me, and who had even more so failed my son. I expressed my feeling on the importance of listening to someone when they are asking for help and not to just dismiss it out of hand. I've lost my baby boy and there was no way I was going to sit back and allow this to happen...I wanted answers.

Chapter Three

On 9 September 2021, my life was about to change forever, although I didn't know it yet. I got up and got ready for work. I was still staying at Naomi's with Mero. It was Mero's first day starting college doing a catering course at Altrincham College. Before I left, I went into the bedroom where Mero was sleeping. I woke him up, sorted out an Uber for him, I told him to have a good first day and that I loved him, and left him some dinner money. Then off I went to work. I was working as a teaching assistant at a primary school in Fallowfield at the time. It was a cold day. I remember thinking so when I got in my car and looked at the temperature gauge. The steering wheel was also cold, and I had to rub my hands together to warm them.

During the day I was telling my friends how proud I was of Mero going to college, because he was kicked out of school when he was fourteen years old for being caught with weed on him. At the time I was annoyed with the school, because instead of delving deeper into the circumstances, for example asking Mero if there was anything happening at home. He was excluded and offered a place in a school PRU. Errol and I refused, and we paid for home schooling instead. Twice a week he went to Explore Learning in Didsbury. I would take him when I finished work on Tuesday and Thursday. It was hard and tiring, but I knew it was what I had to. Had the school conducted a thorough investigation, they would have given Mero the help and support he so obviously needed. At the time he was kicked out, his nana Eldora had passed away and he was struggling with her death because they had a beautiful relationship, where he would visit her each week, and she would spoil him with all of his favourite foods.

When Errol and I split up, our home was never the same, and then Remi moved out to live with his girlfriend Sadie. These were massive changes that happened in a short space of time. Mero went from seeing his dad every day, to seeing him as and when, and he realised he was no longer a priority in his dad's life, and I had to become both mother and father to our boys. The breakdown of our relationship had a negative effect on Mero, and for the next six months, he didn't see his dad, which was when Mero needed him the most. Sadly, to say, their relationship never recovered, and they grew apart. Mero wouldn't let it go, refusing to forgive him, and often telling his dad that he had abandoned them for six months.

When I was eating lunch, I received a text from Mero, saying he had sat in the wrong lesson for over thirty minutes, and he didn't realise. I laughed; this was Mero all over. I asked where he was now, and he told me he was in the right lesson. He then asked if he could go to his friends after college. I said he could, and I finished my lunch and went back to work. I ran an after-school club, so on this day I didn't finish work until 5:15pm. As I was driving down Princess Parkway on my way back to my sister's, my phone rang. I put it on loudspeaker. It was a modelling agency, saying that Mero had sent them some pictures and they were interested in working with him. I said I will speak to Mero as soon as he comes in and we will arrange a day to come down, and the lady replied that that was fine, and she looked forward to seeing us both. The call ended by the time I reached Naomi's house, and when I got in, I took my coat off and threw myself down on the settee. She asked me how my day at work went. 'Good,' I replied, and told her about the modelling agency phoning for Mero. We both smiled and said: 'Check out Mero!' I was both proud and surprised that Mero had put himself forward for modelling, especially because he had done it all by himself, which was showing me my baby was growing up.

Naomi then went upstairs. The dinner was on, but I wasn't hungry because I had some sandwiches left over from the after-school club. My phone rang. The reception was bad in the house, and I could just about hear the mum of one of Mero's friends, who said Mero had been stabbed. There was panic and fear in her voice, whereas I was so calm. 'Where is he?' I asked. 'All I know is somewhere in Old Trafford,' she replied. I put the phone down and went to the bottom of the stairs and shouted: 'Mero's been stabbed!' My sister ran downstairs, quickly followed by her boyfriend. We got into her car, and I told her to just drive to Old Trafford. We didn't know where we were going; we were just driving. I was still so calm at this point. In my head, I was telling myself my baby will be okay. I phoned Errol, who told me he too was out driving looking for Mero.

We were driving down Chorlton Road, in the Whalley Range area, near the Whalley pub, and all I could see were flashing lights from the police cars that were at the scene. The road was taped off from the traffic lights. It was like a scene from a film, and seeing this, my heart literally stopped beating in my chest. I screamed at Naomi to stop the car. I jumped out and ran over to the ambulance, I was screaming, 'It's my son, let me in!' However, the ambulance driver just drove off. I then ran over to the police officer who was standing by the tape. 'Where have they taken my son?' I shouted. He replied, 'I don't know.' I thought that he was cold and unhelpful, like he couldn't be bothered. I ran back to my sister's car, and we tried to follow the ambulance, but we lost sight of it, because we were trying to drive through rush hour traffic.

It was at that moment when it came back to me. After my sister Marie had passed away, I went to see a psychic in Bolton. When we pulled up outside the bungalow, we were greeted by a man in a wheelchair. I went in first, sat down in the living room and had my reading. Nothing much was resonating with me, apart from when he told me about the canvas picture I had in my living room of my sister. As my reading was coming to an end, Mero came in and asked if he could use the toilet. He was seven years old at the time. The man looked at him and asked me who he was. I told him he was my son. He then looked at me and said that he could see blue flashing lights all around him. I smiled and said he loves music, thinking that this would be camera lights. I never thought in a million years that this was going to be my son's last day on earth. Flashing lights is all I could see, and I knew from then my baby wasn't going to be okay. Despite this I held onto every bit of hope I had left in me.

With us being in Old Trafford, I thought the ambulance was going to take Mero to Trafford General, so I told Naomi to drive there. At the same time, I called Errol and Remi, telling them to get to the Royal Infirmary, as I didn't want Mero to be alone. When we arrived at Trafford General, we asked the receptionist if Rhamero West had been brought to the hospital, and when he replied that he hadn't, my heart sank, because I knew for certain that my baby wasn't okay. I screamed at Naomi to take me to the Royal Infirmary. The traffic was horrendous, and she was driving fast, going through red lights trying to get us over there fast. Through my tears, I began to hyperventilate, and I couldn't catch my breath. 'I can't breathe,' I gasped to my sister. She began to do breathe work and encouraged me to copy her. My hands suddenly locked together, and pains were shooting across my chest. I felt as if I was having a stroke, but I knew that the shock was preparing my body to go into panic mode.

Driving from Trafford to the Royal Infirmary felt like hours, like time had stopped, and during the journey, Errol kept phoning, asking how far away I was. 'Ten minutes away,' we said. We had the phone on loudspeaker, and only had five percent battery power left. By the time we arrived at Upper Brook Street, waiting to turn right towards the hospital, only minutes away, my phone rang. 'Kelly,' Errol said. 'Yes,' I replied. 'He's gone.' I opened my mouth and the scream that came out was from the depths of my soul. We finally pulled up outside the hospital and I got out of the car and ran.

As I sprinted to the hospital, all I could think was that I wanted to be with my baby, even though I knew that he had gone. I wanted him to know that Mummy was there with him. The doors to the hospital opened automatically and when I went through, I saw Remi. Mero was in an emergency room that was lit brightly. Doctors as well as police were in the room, and Errol was sitting on a chair next to the bed. The atmosphere in the room felt eerie and quiet. No one was speaking. Mero was lying on a bed surrounded by chairs and emergency equipment. There was blood on the floor, and near his cheek. To me he looked like he was just asleep. He was dressed in a black hoodie, a white t-shirt, black North Face pants and grey Nike trainers.

When I saw my baby boy lying there, lifeless on the bed, it was soul destroying; it would be for any mother. I screamed, unable to breathe. The doctor told me to sit down and to control my breathing. When Naomi rushed in, she fell to the floor when she saw Mero, because she was like a second mum to him, treating him like her own son. I took a chair next to Mero's bed, only to be told by a police officer that I couldn't touch my son, because they needed to take forensic samples from him. I cried and stroked his eyebrow and kissed his cold forehead, while Errol and his brother Remi stood silently and looked on. My mum came into the room, and she cried when she saw Mero. I looked at the officer and said to them; 'They had better find who has done this to my baby.'

I phoned my best friend Gaynor. I cried down the phone telling her that they had taken my baby, he's dead. Gaynor became frantic and asked where I was.

I told her I was at the hospital, and then hung up and phoned my other friend Karla, but she didn't answer, so I phoned Jo, a friend of hers, and asked her to go and tell Karla that Mero had been murdered. I then phoned my friend Nicola, and through my tears, all I could say was, 'Mero is dead.'

After being with Mero, I had to get some fresh air. I felt as if I was in a daze, like I was in a movie. When I reached the doors, family and friends had gathered there. The shock and disbelief were on their faces, just as it was on mine, it was unimaginable. As I stood there, with people around me, I didn't want to be touched; I didn't want anyone to hug me. I remember my niece, Deanne, coming out of the hospital after seeing Mero and overcome by grief, she dropped to the floor and cried.

The police were all over the hospital, and I was called into a side room by a detective wanting to ask me questions about this morning. I told her I had woken him up, sorted him an Uber to get to college, and then I went to work. I even showed them the texts I had received from Mero during the day. They wanted as much information in detail as I could give them. I was in the room for an hour approximately, answering their questions. After the questioning, I was told Mero's body would be transported to the Coroner's Office in Oldham, where they deal with the bodies of murder victims. They were going to carry out two biopsy procedures to collect evidence to be used in court if needed. I was informed this could take up to six weeks, and I was also told the police would contact me if any new information arose, and that I should pass on to them straightaway any information I was given.

Then a doctor came in and told me they would be moving Mero into another room so that family could see him. When they wheeled him out on the stretcher to the side room, I was standing at the doors. I didn't want everyone to see Mero in that way, so I only allowed a select few in to see him. I went in and sat beside my boy. When I tried to touch his face, again they said that I couldn't touch him because he was part of a crime scene, so I then stroked his eyebrows. I thought that this at least was acceptable, because they didn't say that I couldn't do that.

I didn't want to leave his side. I couldn't bring myself to accept that this was happening. When it was time to leave the hospital, I said goodbye to a few family members. Errol gave me a hug, and so did Remi, who was staying with Sadie. I went back to my sister's house, and I went straight to the room where Mero had slept. I took his duvet blanket and brought it to my bedroom. I didn't even have the energy to shower. I plugged my phone into the charger, and it was pinging all night with messages from my friends and family. I ignored them and wrapped myself up in the blanket Mero had last used. I could still smell his scent all over it, and I just lay there and cried. Naomi came into the room and asked if I wanted her to sleep with me. I said yes and she got in the bed and held me. Not surprisingly, I didn't sleep much that night.

The next day I got up, washed, and dressed and went home. I couldn't bring myself to go into Mero's room, so I kept the door closed. It was too painful to go into his room; it was easier to just close the door. I felt so numb, like I was trapped in a movie that I might never be able to escape. Later the same day I was sitting in my small armchair, in my living room when my friends Karla and Nicola came round. They told me they were letting everyone know what had happened to Mero. My work colleagues, who were friends as well as having taught Mero in the past, cried when they were told the news. My doctor phoned, the police had told them what had happened, and they prescribed sleeping tablets and anti-anxiety medication. I'm not usually one to take any medication, but after I'd received the shocking news that I had, the medication the doctor prescribed helped. I couldn't sleep, was constantly on edge, and having flashbacks and my anxiety went through the roof. I had the television on and when the six o'clock news came on, all I could see were pictures of Mero and them talking about his murder. I later emailed my local councillor and told her that Mero was dead, nothing else.

Family, friends, neighbours, and even people from the community were coming to the house with food, shopping, and flowers for Mero. I put a gazebo up outside the front of the house, for people to lay their flowers and to light a candle. It was more somewhere for Mero's friends to be able to remember him. My garden was covered with flowers, lights, and balloons, all for my baby boy. I still felt like it was a bad dream and that I would wake up from it all. My appetite disappeared, through the stress I was experiencing, and the weight began to fall away. I had family and friends around me every single day, but at the same time I still felt lonely. It was like I was doing it all on my own, like no one would ever understand the pain and loss I was going through. It was hard reading the hundreds of heartfelt messages, because it meant that I was finally forced to accept this nightmare as my actual reality.

From the start I had been receiving messages from people giving me the names of the ones responsible for my baby's death, and all of the information I received, I passed straight on to the police. Ryan Cashin, Marquis Richards, Xavier Wynter and Giovanni Lawrence were the names that I had been given as those who were responsible for Mero's murder. I didn't know any of the boys personally, but I had grown up with Junior Richards, Marquis's dad, when I lived in Moss Side at the age of six or seven, then we moved to Fallowfield. I was thoroughly disgusted when I heard it was Junior's son. I also found out that Keliah was Marquis's mum. I had also known her from growing up in Moss Side. I was disappointed that she knew me and where I lived, but never once did she reach out to me.

The officer dealing with my case was Liz Hopkinson. She came round a few days later. Liz kept me up to date with all the information the police were receiving. I trusted her straightaway, because she had been successful in solving numerous cases in Manchester. I'd previously watched a documentary on this. Liz was well dressed in a dark grey pants suit, her eyes were brown, and her hair was of medium length, and pinned up. When she was leaving, she asked if I had any questions. 'Yes,' I replied. 'Please, just find who has done this to my boy.' She looked at me and hugged me and said: 'I promise I will.'

Every day since Mero's passing my house was always full of visitors, coming to check I was okay, and eating. Mero's birthday was coming up, he would have been seventeen, and it was heart-breaking that he was never going to see it. We wanted to give him the party he would have had if he had lived. Seeing his face all over the news made me feel low and depressed, and made me realise how I was still having difficulty coming to terms with his death. So, my friends and family rallied round and helped organise the best party for him, given the circumstances. Now, I'm usually a woman whose very house proud, but I found now I wasn't even bothered by the mess the party was creating.

On 16 September, Tracey, the liaison officer, visited and told me that Marquis Richards had been arrested and charged with murder. I was relieved that one of them had been caught as quickly as he had. I was grateful to all of those who had messaged me giving me the names and blessed that the investigation was moving on. But I was still angry and would not be happy until everyone involved in taking Mero's life was caught and then brought to justice. I phoned Naomi, who was at work, and cried as I told her the news, and when I told Remi, he said that he didn't want to know until they were all caught. When I phoned Errol, he was just silent on the other end of the line. Later that day, I was at home with Karla and Nicola, who both wanted to hug me, but I held them off, saying, 'Please don't.' I just needed time to take it all in and to begin processing all of the information I'd been bombarded with over the last few days. Naomi came by after work and she asked me if I was okay, 'I just want them all,' I replied.

For Mero's birthday we decorated the garden with 17th balloons and photographs of Mero. I had a flag made with Mero's photograph on it and hung it on the front of the house. Friends and family brought food, and we even had a deejay who set up in the garden. The party had been advertised on Facebook, inviting Mero's friends to come and celebrate in his memory. We had the biggest party ever on this day, 20 September 2021. It was like a mini carnival, and not only was my house and garden full of people, but also the road and the avenue too. Everyone ate and drank, and we partied into the early hours for Mero. Both Mero's and Remi's friends had brought fireworks, and we lit up Fallowfield. Watching the fireworks was emotional. We put messages into lanterns and shouted, 'We love you, Mero!' and let them drift up into the sky. Looking up, all I could think was, *my baby is now in heaven*. I wanted to brighten up the whole damn sky for him.

I found myself staring at the faces of the people who had come to help us celebrate Mero's birthday, and kept wondering, *is this really happening?* It felt as if I wasn't fully present. I still didn't allow people to hug me. I guess the reason I was holding a part of me back, was that I feared crying, and never being able to stop. In the early hours of the morning, I finally went to bed. My friend Neffie and her daughters stayed over. Tari slept in my bed with me, while Neffie and her other daughter Nubia slept in Mero's room. After staying in his room for about thirty minutes, they felt spooked and came into my room and slept on the floor. My friends Sandra, Paula and Gaynor also stayed over, and after only a few hours' sleep, we got up and set about cleaning my house, as well as the road, and the avenue, which were all very messy after the party. Mero's auntie Suzette also came round and joined in with the cleaning up, and once we finished, we sat in the front garden because it was a warm day. Sandra went to get us some food from the chippy, and when she returned, she told us she got the food for free because the woman in the takeaway had heard what had happened to Mero.

People were always telling me how strong I was. However, seeing my eldest son Remi breakdown and cry was hard, knowing that he has to live with seeing his younger brother with his chest open, while the doctors were trying to save him. If I'd have seen that, I would have probably broken down like my son. Waking up and seeing Mero's friends coming to my house every day, sitting in the garden from morning until night, grieving over their loss, broke my heart. They were just kids themselves, trying to take in what had happened. For the first month I needed the sleeping tablets and the anti-anxiety medications the doctor had prescribed. Hearing nothing from the police regarding the boys who had taken Mero's life was hell, as well as not being able to organise his funeral, because I was waiting for his body to be released by the coroner. It was all getting too much for me. I was crying myself to sleep each night, so I decided to get away for a couple of days and go to a spa hotel with my sister.

I had to get away from Fallowfield, as I was in information overload; I was absorbing everything going on around me. We went to The Mere in Knutsford. My sister understands me well; if I am quiet, she won't question anything, she will just go at my pace. Our room in the hotel was beautiful. We dropped our bags and lay down on our beds and ate crisps and sweets and put face masks on and chilled until it was dinner time. The restaurant we were booked into was called Browns and we giggled, because that is our surname, and I have this belief that everything was meant to be. We ordered steak and chips, which was delicious. Afterwards we had an early night, and I took a sleeping tablet and went to sleep.

The next morning, we had breakfast, and our friend Madeeha drove down to see us. We went for a walk around the forest that surrounded the hotel. I was there physically but mentally I had checked out. We walked for about an hour, and chatted about general stuff, to give me a break and to help me clear my head, which was spinning out of control with so many thoughts. We were taking in the beautiful scenery as we walked, and we talked about having some Reiki. Madeeha is a Reiki practitioner, and she said she would give me a session once I felt up to having it. Madeeha then left and Naomi and I went to the spa. Lying down on the hot stone bed was just what I needed. It helped me to ground myself and be fully present. We took full advantage of the facilities, and after a few hours we went back to our room in our dressing gowns. We relaxed and watched television that evening, but the thought of knowing that I had to leave in the morning and return to face the situation I had left was hard. In bed that night, and each night since, I talked to Mero, asking him to help catch the boys who had taken his life. The next day we drove back to my house.

Chapter Four

As soon as I got home my friend Karla came round. She and my sister had both been my rock since it all happened. She always brought a sandwich and a drink with her to make sure I was looking after myself. Mero's friends were still coming round, and they would sit under the gazebo. They would also ask if I was okay, and if they could do anything for me. I couldn't even have my grandson, Caerus, over because I wasn't in the right frame of mind. Sitting in my living room with Karla and other friends and family coming in and out of my house was my way of coping with the situation. Having people around helped me keep busy. I suppose it kept my mind distracted from what was happening, which was the sad reality that my boy's life had been taken in such a cruel way.

That night when I went to bed, for the first ever time I dreamed of Mero. In the dream I couldn't see him; he was on the phone, and he clearly said: 'Mum, can I get some chicken from Dallas?' This was his favourite food shop. I said yes and he replied that he was going home now. As he said that, I saw a bright light with loads of people standing near to it. I couldn't see who they were because the light was so bright, all I could make out were their outlines. I woke up crying, hearing my baby say he was going home broke me again. I messaged my friend Madeeha and told her about the dream. She is a spiritual person, and she explained that the people could be Mero's loved ones who had passed on, like my sister Marie, and Mero's nana. For the next two days, the dream physically and emotionally took it out of me. Hearing his voice so clear meant so much, but when he said he was going home, all I could think was home is with me and your brother.

It was frustrating that I'd still not heard anything from the police, apart from Tracey, my liaison officer, who was amazing. The silence made me feel so helpless, angry, and upset that there didn't seem to be any progress or updates. To cope with these feelings, I would go and stay at Naomi's house to get away from it all and come back home in the morning. It was hard to talk to Remi in any depth about how we were both feeling and what was happening with the investigation. Although we were being strong for each other, I knew as Mero's big brother, he was feeling the devastating loss just as much as I was, and to add to it, he was also worried about me, and how I was coping. I came to realise quickly that he would only talk about Mero when he wanted to, and I had to respect his boundaries. Not being able to speak freely with Remi made me feel anxious for his safety when he wasn't at home, and I began to feel anxious and would cry. I was still relying on the medication my doctor prescribed and could only eat small amounts of food.

Remi came in one day and said, 'Mum, can I have a dog?' How could I ever say no after what he had gone through? Even though I wasn't a pet lover, I said he could, and within an hour Remi came home with an XL Bully puppy. Looking at the dog, I said there was no way it was a puppy, because of how big he was. Remi laughed and insisted it was a puppy. I only allowed him to keep the dog if I could name it. My friends Jo and Karla brought me a star when Mero passed away and the star was called Draco. I thought the name really suited the dog so much. Draco has a light grey and blue-coloured coat. He was so shy and nervous when we first got him, and at times I was thinking, *what have I done?* But it was seeing Remi smile, that's all that mattered to me.

Tracey finally contacted me and told me I could start the process of organising Mero's funeral. Although I was eager for any news, it still felt like a heavy blow to my stomach, knowing that I now had to start making plans to bury my baby boy. I had no idea where to start. A friend Mandy recommended Kane's Funeral Services, and Helen Ryan Lewis, the funeral director, arranged to come out to see us. I was clear from the beginning that I didn't want anyone else organising the arrangements, other than Errol, Remi, and me. I wanted it to be special for Mero. Helen duly visited and showed us various samples of horses and carriages, and the coffins we could choose from.

As Errol and I were talking, I asked him who the boy was, the one who sat in my garden every day, and Errol replied that he was Mero's friend and was with him at the time of the stabbing. I didn't know that, as I hadn't met him before. Errol suddenly turned to me and asked me if I knew what Mero's last words were. I looked at Errol and Helen and said that I didn't know. Errol was hesitating to tell me, but then he said that Mero had told the boy, the same one sitting outside my house to call his mum. At that moment I felt like my heart was being squeezed, and I broke down and cried. Errol came to sit next to me, and Helen made her excuses, saying that she would come back another day. Before she went, she left a book for us to look through. Hearing your son's last words, hearing all he wanted was me, his mum, destroyed me. Errol stayed with me for a few hours, and then he too left. Even though we had split up two years prior to losing Mero, we remained friends.

Annette, my dad's wife, who I have a good relationship with phoned, offering a night's stay for two people in a hotel in Blackpool. I replied that I would like to go. My niece D'mornae, who was my little rock, agreed to come with me, and I drove us down. We pulled up outside the hotel. It was so cold being by the sea, but I was happy to be getting away from it all. I was so jumpy at the time, and I screamed because I saw what I thought was a mouse running past us, but we laughed when we realised it was just a leaf blowing on the pavement. A couple who was passing us laughed too. It was good to get away to a place where I was anonymous, where no one knew what I was going through. D'mornae and I gave each other dares to do, while we were waiting for the receptionist, the phone rang, and I dared D'mornae to answer the phone and pretend to be the receptionist. She went behind the desk and lifted the receiver. She took the room service order and said thank you and put the phone down. We were in stitches, and we never got caught. We had such a laugh, which was what I needed, and once we had checked in and were in our room, we lay on our beds and reminisced about Mero, and we laughed and cried.

While we were watching television my phone rang. The call was from a number I didn't know. I said: 'Hello.' And the detective, Paul Davies, asked if I could hear him. I replied that I could, and he then proceeded to tell me that they had made another arrest. I made the intention to stay calm, because I didn't want to miss a single word. I wanted to hear everything he had to say. 'We've arrested Ryan Cashin,' he said. He then went on to say they had twenty-four hours to charge them, and that they were waiting to hear from the CPS on this. He also advised me to keep my phone on and to wait. When I ended the call, my heart was racing, and when I told D'mornae what the detective had said, we jumped around the hotel room, hugging each other. I took a sleeping tablet to help me sleep, because I was too hyped up from the news of the arrests.

In the early hours of the morning, I received another phone call from Paul, who told me the CPS had agreed to charge them with murder. I couldn't speak; I was overcome with the knowledge that they were going to be charged with my baby's murder. I phoned Naomi, Remi and Errol telling them of the news - D'mornae said she would let the rest of the family know, who were now relieved by the current action. The whole process has destroyed me inside, but I knew I had to fight this for my baby boy. Before driving back to Manchester the next day, we had our breakfast and were ready to come home, especially after the news I'd received. On the drive home, I got a flat tyre, and had to drive slowly through country lanes, looking for a garage. After about five minutes we found a garage, but they didn't have my tyre size, and I asked them to put any size on, as it was just to get me home, and I promised the mechanic I would get it sorted out when I got back to Manchester.

My life had changed forever. It was now like a roller coaster. I had no clue as to what was coming next, let alone which emotions I was going to have to face. I continued to talk to Mero, asking him to give me the strength and guidance to move forward. I never thought my life would turn out like this. I went from being a mum of two boys, now of one, and working full-time in a school, to a grieving mother, who was struggling to accept that my son had been murdered. Going back to work was the least of my worries, as I didn't want to leave the house. I didn't have the drive to do anything, apart from put on a brave face every day. My boss contacted me, asking when I was going back to work; I told him I wasn't returning to work until after the court case.

Knowing that I had a funeral to organise, I brought myself a writing pad. I wanted to make notes of the meetings with Errol and Remi. We were determined we were going to have it how we wanted it to be. The colour theme of the funeral was going to be purple, which was Mero's favourite colour, as well as blue and white. I got in touch again with Helen to tell her we had chosen a white coffin and four horses and carriage. Helen got in touch with Holy Trinity Church on Platt Lane; this was the church where we had Mero blessed as a baby. They agreed to have Mero's service there and gave us a date of 22 October 2021. I had to sit Remi down and ask if he was okay with this date, as the day before was his birthday. He reassured me that he was fine with this and so we went ahead with that date. I wanted the funeral to be perfect for my baby boy. I had it all sorted, from the food, flowers, venue - being the Burnage Cricket Club where we were going to hold the wake and the funeral reception - and the deejay. I looked through all of Mero's photographs, and picked out my favourite ones that would go in the Order of Service. Keena, Errol's cousin, and her mum Hildred, Errol's aunt, insisted they wanted to pay for it, and I was so grateful that they offered to do this for us.

Helen phoned me a couple of days later and asked if I'd like to see Mero, who was now lying in a chapel of rest. I said that I would, and when I asked Errol and Remi, they said that they couldn't do it. I asked my sister, and she agreed to come with me. Helen drove us to the chapel of rest. Before we went into the viewing room, we were asked to wait for a minute, and Naomi asked if I was okay, I said that I was. A lady came and took us to a door. Knowing that my baby was on the other side made my knees go weak. I took a deep breath and willed myself to walk into the room. It was cold, and in the middle my baby boy was lying in a white coffin, with white netting over it. I looked at him, and then had to quickly look away, and then I cried. Naomi hugged me, and said, 'Come on,' and we both approached the coffin slowly, and we both had a little cry.

I then removed the netting to look at him. Mero was dressed in the black Armani tracksuit that I had bought him for his upcoming seventeenth birthday. I held his hand and kissed him on his forehead. Naomi held his other hand, and we reminisced about the good times, while trying to take it all in. His skin was cold to my touch and was a grey, ashy colour, and as I looked down on his face, I commented that his nose seemed thinner; it now looked more like my nose, rather than his dad's. We stayed with him for about thirty minutes. On the way home Errol called, asking how I was, and he said I was so strong going to see him, but I wanted to; I had to. Although I was happy, I saw Mero, I was sad and broken inside. Remi was waiting at home when I returned and he hugged me, knowing where I'd just been. The next day, we were presented with Mero's handprints and four locks of his hair by the liaison officers, and later I had Mero's handprints framed as a keepsake for us.

Family and friends were still at my house as I was sorting things out for the wake. I topped up my tan and had my eyelashes done to make myself feel a bit better. I wore jeans with a white t-shirt with Mero's face printed on it. I took a taxi to the Cricket Club. The deejay and I were the first ones there, and slowly and surely people started coming in. The room was filled with so much love, and we had a drink and a dance for our baby boy. It finished around midnight, and then a few people came back to my house afterwards, where we listened to music and had a few more drinks, and I didn't get to bed until after three o'clock in the morning.

At six o'clock that evening, we were able to get into the venue and set things up before the funeral the next day. I met my friends and family, and we all worked together to make the room look special for my little prince. We had white tables and chairs, with purple ribbon on the backs of the chairs. There was a blue strip running in the middle of the tables, and for the centre piece we had twig trees with purple balloons attached to them, with Mero's name on the balloons, and with pictures of Mero dangling from the branches. On the stage was Mero's name lit up in lights, with purple, white and blue balloons surrounding the letters. There were earth balloons on the ceiling celebrating 'Mero's World'. Behind the memory table there were music notes decorating the backdrop because Mero loved music. We hung the flag that was printed with Mero's photograph on it next to his table, and there were party favours and candles for the guests to take with them. The love everybody had put into the room to make it was perfect was wonderful, and I was happy with the result, but heartbroken that this was happening to my baby boy. He was only sixteen, and he shouldn't have been taken away from us in this way.

Planning for Mero's funeral was overwhelming, but I had to remain strong. I wanted it to be a good and memorable evening for everyone. Inside, I was feeling numb and lonely, but I kept a brave smile on my face. Every time I was asked if I was okay, I would just reply 'Yes', but deep down I wasn't and didn't think anyone could understand my pain and loss as a mother. Only Errol could, because we were connected through our child Mero. Although I understood he was grieving himself, he certainly wasn't supportive in the way I needed him to be.

The day of the funeral, 22 October, finally arrived. I woke up early and Errol was the first to come to the house. Sadie, my daughter-in-law, came with our grandson, Caerus. He needed to get dressed in his suit. People began arriving because Mero was coming home before we went on to the church, and it was then Errol asked me to help with Caerus, but at the time he asked, I looked outside and I said, 'No, my boy is here.' I walked downstairs and outside and stood in a daze looking at the coffin and the horses and carriage. People approached me and tried to hug me, but I told them not to hug me, because I was okay. Deep down I knew that if I was being hugged all day, then I would just break. The mourners who gathered outside the house looked beautiful, all wearing hints of purple for Mero.

Once we were ready, we set off walking behind the horse and carriage to the church on Platt Lane. I never looked back once. I just kept staring straight ahead, looking at my baby boy, while holding on to Remi's hand. Behind us, the mourners were letting off purple flares and playing music. The traffic had to be held up for us as we filled the road. The day was very cold, and as we turned right onto Platt Lane towards the church, at last I glanced behind me at the people walking behind me, and it just went to show how loved my son was. We pulled up outside the church, and there were more mourners standing in silence. My stepdad, Errol, Remi, Damien, Mark, and Marley carried Mero into the church.

The service was so well-attended that the church couldn't hold everyone inside. I sat at the front of the church with Errol and Remi, while Naomi and Damien sat behind us. Remi broke down and cried in the church. God only knows how broken he is now his only brother is gone. The service was beautiful, with family members and friends standing up and talking about Mero, whose coffin was covered with the flag made up of different pictures of him on it. We chose three songs for Mero: Remi's choice was Lil Durk's 'Fabricated', which played as Mero's coffin entered the church; 'Baby Boy' by Felicia Adams, my choice, was played during the service, and Mary J Blige's 'Everything', which Errol had chosen, was played when we left the church.

The whole thing lasted for just an hour, and during it I was holding back my tears, and I wore sunglasses so no one could see my eyes. I felt as if I was there, but I wasn't, like I was going to wake up from it all. After the church, we got into the funeral cars and drove to the cemetery. Remi had hired a flashy car, just for Mero. He wanted to make the event special and for him to have his little part in it. The drive to the cemetery was long and family and friends were stopping the traffic to make the convoy go as smoothly as possible. Karla, Nicola, and a few of the girls arrived at the cemetery first to pick up the balloons for me, which were going to be released afterwards.

When we arrived at the cemetery, Remi was already there in the hire car. I got out of the funeral car and walked across the grass and looked down into the empty grave. The crowds gathered around me at the graveside, and Mark, my stepdad, Marley, Remi, Errol, and Damien brought the coffin to the grave. All I could do was just stare at the coffin as they placed it down. It was cold, and it began to rain, I was wearing a white dress, and I was so cold and couldn't stop shaking. The priest conducted the service and then Diyari, Chace and I released six white doves into the grey skies. One by one the mourners helped to fill in the grave, laying earth on Mero's coffin that was covered with single roses. I felt so lost and empty; the one day I needed my baby's father to be there for me, and he wasn't. He stood on one side of the grave, and I stood at the other with Remi. I'd have thought the twenty-six years we were together would have stood for something. To have no support from the father of my children when I needed it most was heart-breaking. It was my brother-in-law, Damien, who came to me and put his arm around me.

Once the grave was filled in, it was then covered with an array of beautiful flowers and pictures of Mero. Mero's special day was filmed so I had it forever. We released the balloons and set the fireworks off. The rain was coming down heavily now, and we got back into our cars and went to the venue. I remember being in the car with D'mornae and having a shot of rum to warm my body up. Outside the Cricket Club, people hugged me, and somehow, I found the strength to stay strong and we partied for my boy. The rooms looked lovely and the energy and love for him was amazing. We had food and two deejays played in two separate rooms: one for Mero's friends and the other for the grown-ups. People came in and out throughout the day. The food was set up in the corner of the room. Sandra and other helpers were serving hot soup first to warm everyone after standing out in the cold for so long. Family and Mero's friends sat down at the reserved tables, and others were filled with those wanting to pay their respects. The catering was provided by Silverspoon, Karla and Nicola helped to serve the food to the guests, and once everyone had eaten, I got on the mic and asked Sandra, Naomi, Karla, and Nicola to come to the front, where I presented each of them with a bouquet of flowers, thanking them for all their help. We then partied the night away. At eleven o'clock, we let off some more fireworks to say our final goodbyes to Mero, and shortly after that Remi and I got a taxi home. I was tired and went straight to bed, whereas Remi stayed up with a couple of his friends.

Chapter Five

After the funeral I decided I needed counselling. Work arranged for me to have some, but I didn't feel the counsellor was any good. She didn't talk to me and there was an awkward atmosphere between us; plus, I didn't feel a connection to her, so I wasn't able to open up and say what I was feeling inside. So, I applied online to a company. I completed the form and was accepted straightaway. I had weekly sessions over Facetime with a woman called Roslyne. At first, I wouldn't open up, I was scared to. However, over the coming weeks Roslyne persevered, and in our sessions, she began to make me feel comfortable enough to be able to open up and to finally express what I was feeling inside.

Like an onion, she peeled back each of the layers I had built up with Mero's death, as well as the layers I had built up before that. Roslyne would ask me questions and my reply would be to ask her why she'd just asked me that. I had a fear of opening up and to talk about how I was *really* feeling. This came from not having any one I could confide in when I was growing up, so I would hold things in until I couldn't hold onto them any longer, then I would explode, like a volcano, to release my emotions.

One important question she asked was: Who was Kelly Brown? She said to take away being a partner, mother, daughter, sister, and auntie. Who is Kelly? I paused because I couldn't answer. I cried because I had lost my identity. I had lost the person I once was; it had all been stripped from me. I replied that I didn't know who Kelly was. Roslyne then said that we needed to find Kelly again. She then went on to ask questions to do with things I liked, and enjoyed doing etc. During some sessions all I would do was cry all the way through. Things slowly started to get better, and on some level, I was able to accept Mero's death, but on others I struggled with the cruel way in which he was taken from me. I know I will never be the same person I was before I lost Mero; a large part of Kelly died with him. Now I was no longer afraid of verbalising what was on my mind, which made me feel much better than holding onto what was inside.

One morning when I woke up, I decided that I was going to turn my pain into a fight. I needed to fight for justice for my baby boy and to raise awareness of the devastating consequences of knife crime. A part of me died the day Mero was taken, and I knew that my life had changed forever, as it would change without my son. I decided that I wasn't going to be that quiet Kelly, the woman who wouldn't speak up for herself and was too shy to speak in public. Through the death and grieving process, I had found my voice, and I was determined that everyone was going to hear me.

On 9 November, just two months after Mero's passing, I came up with the idea of planning a march to Norton Street in Old Trafford. I put a post on Facebook asking for people to support me on the march. I asked that the people who wanted to come along meet at my house at five o'clock, so that we could arrive at Norton Street at six thirty-six, the exact time Mero passed away. The turnout was amazing. We carried banners which said, 'Justice for Mero', as well as purple glow sticks, as purple was his favourite colour, and family and friends and people from the local community were even wearing jumpers with Mero's picture on them.

We left my house on Bucklow Avenue in Fallowfield, the area where Mero grew up and knew the streets well. Claire, my cousin, had a megaphone and she was shouting: 'Whose world, is it?' And we replied: 'Mero's world'. She then said: 'Put down the knives,' to which we replied: 'Save all lives.' We shouted this all the way. People were coming out of shops, and kids were looking out of their windows as we passed by. Our route took us down Hart Road. We turned right onto Lloyd Street, left onto Claremont Road, and down to the end. We passed Alexander Park, and went on to Withington Road, towards the Whalley Pub. There were family members in cars at the beginning and the end of the procession beeping their horns which lifted our energy and made our voices louder.

I knew we were getting closer to the spot where Mero had been stabbed once we turned left onto Upper Chorlton Road. My heart was hammering in my chest, and I started having horrifying visions of Mero running through the streets, trying to get away from his attackers. We turned left onto Norton Street and in the distance, I could see some people standing at the spot, and candles that had been placed on the ground. As soon as we reached the spot a blanket of silence descended upon us. Our voices were silenced. I stepped forward and placed a lantern down, with some flowers, and Naomi helped me attach a picture of Mero to the wall. I asked for a minute's silence for Mero. We all bowed our heads, and in the following silence you could hear the proverbial pin drop. That minute felt more like it had stretched to twenty minutes. After the silence I was introduced to Kate, Caron, and Maggie, three strong and amazing women who were with my baby until help arrived. I held onto each of them in turn and cried. As Mero's mum, I couldn't thank them enough for being there for my son. In all we stayed at Norton Street for thirty minutes, but then I had to leave, as the terrible realisation that this was the street where my son's life was taken was dawning on me, but before I left I exchanged numbers with the ladies and asked if we could meet, because I desperately wanted to learn as many details as possible of that day that I could.

Off we went back down Norton Street, and Claire linked arms with me, still shouting: 'Whose world, is it?' into the megaphone. When we arrived back at my house, we stood in the garden, and I thanked everyone for their support. They all drifted away until only Remi's and Mero's friends remained sitting under the gazebo. I was exhausted, the walk and the emotion of being in the actual spot where Mero was attacked really took it out of me, so I went to bed, took a sleeping tablet, and cried myself to sleep. Prior to the march, I had never wanted to go to Norton Street, to visit the place where Mero met his death; it was too painful to think that was where my baby was hurt.

After the march I arranged a meeting with the Violence Reduction Unit. I went with my niece Deanne and my sister Naomi. There we met Dan and Mel, and we expressed our concerns around knife crime, and I was able to talk about Mero's murder. They told us the policies and procedures they had in place for dealing with and reducing knife crime in Manchester. At the end of the meeting, I understood how much they are doing to tackle knife crime; however, I wasn't satisfied, because I still felt my voice and story needed to be heard, as well as that more action needed to be taken.

Grief, I've come to learn, is a funny thing. You can be up one moment and down the next, without any warning. One thing that has come out of my grief is that I'm now not afraid to cut anyone who isn't good for me out of my life. My mum phoned me after Mero's funeral. She apologised for not being in touch, saying that she'd had a head cold. I was shocked and disgusted; a head cold was a poor excuse for not getting in contact. 'You're acting like Mero's gone on holiday, or something. He's dead, and it takes you a month to contact me?' I said, and I hung up on her. Historically, we've not had the best mother and daughter relationship, and I thought, despite this, she would still be there for me at this sad and desperate time, but I was clearly wrong, and we haven't spoken since.

Another lesson came from Judy, a woman who I considered as my best friend, who wasn't there for me either. She only came to the house a couple of times, and she did come to Mero's seventeenth birthday party with her daughter, Amara, and her parents. She hugged me and said that she didn't know what to say to me, which was understandable. A few days later she came over and we talked about Mero. He had been close to Judy and Amara, and we reminisced at what a joker he was. Judy came to Mero's funeral and attended the first march to Norton Street. After I had expressed to her how I was feeling, we didn't remain close, and we drifted apart. I understand that people come into your life to teach you lessons, and what I gained from my mum, Judy, and Mero's dad, Errol, was to never give up on people who need you.

I messaged Caron and asked if I could meet up with her and the other ladies who helped Mero, and wet met at the Seymour Play Centre. I asked my friend Nicola if she would come with me for support, and I brought my grandson, Caerus, along with me too. Before that, I nipped in to Asda to buy small gifts for them, on behalf of Mero and myself. When we all arrived, we hugged, and I asked each one of them to recount their memories of the day Mero was attacked. From her flat, Maggie recounted that she could hear loads of noise and saw the car Mero was travelling in crashing into a tree. She saw him jump out and then he and his friends being chased. She phoned the police straightaway. At this point, the police were already aware of what was happening, because of the many reports of the situation coming in from members of the public.

A report from another lady who wasn't present, but who had previously told the ladies that she had seen Mero knocking on doors, trying to get away, but no one answered. Then the attacker cornered Mero, saying; 'I've got you now.' And he stabbed him. She called from her bedroom window for the boy to leave Mero alone. He then got in a car and drove off. The lady urged Mero to come across the road to her. He

45

stood up and crossed over and collapsed on her doorstep. Kate added that they found a skipping rope to wrap around his leg to try to stem the bleeding. Caron said she was talking to Mero, asking him the names of his mum and dad, but he was being stubborn and wouldn't say; however, she tried to keep him talking until the ambulance arrived. It was so much information for me to take in. I hugged and thanked them again and we left. On the way to Nicola's, I commented that as much as I was desperate to hear about Mero's last moments from these amazing ladies, the result of it had left me feeling even more numb, lost and empty.

I spoke to my friend Gaynor about the experience, and she suggested a weekend away to Wales. I agreed and the following week we escaped. Thirty minutes away from Wales, Gaynor turned to me and admitted that she had forgotten the key to the caravan. We laughed and drove back to Manchester to pick up the key. By the time we returned to the campsite, it was dark and we couldn't find the caravan. In the end we found it, put our bags down, cooked some food and chilled for the evening. The next day we decided to go to the beach. The weather was cold and windy and we walked for a short distance, and I turned to Gaynor and told her that I wanted to scream. Gaynor had also recently experienced the loss of her partner, and the father of her children. She told me to scream, and that she was also going to scream with me. We took off our shoes and walked into the cold sea and screamed. I opened my mouth and screamed from the pit of my stomach, and released all of the pent-up emotional pain I'd been holding on to.

On the walk back across the sand, we made each other laugh by telling each other stories, and we noticed our feet were covered in a black substance, and we laughed even more because of the mess our feet were in. Back at the caravan, we showered and put our pyjamas on. I cooked steak and potatoes with peppercorn sauce. We had a drink and watched a film, and then had an early night, because we were going home the next day. After being away, it always felt awful to go back home. I was going back to the hell that had become my reality; no son, a court case looming, as well as the first Christmas without Mero.

I felt that Christmas had come around too quickly, and I certainly didn't want to celebrate it. I couldn't bring myself to put up a tree. At one time, I loved Christmas, and my house would light up with the lights and decorations. Instead I had a mural of Mero outside my house. Even though the nights were getting colder, the boys were still coming to the house and sitting under the gazebo, and so to keep them warm I brought out my wood burner. Family and friends were still coming regularly to check on me, making sure that I was eating, and Karla tried to get me out of the house as much as she could. I was taking baby steps moving forward, and I started picking up my goddaughter Pheobe from the school where I used to work, but going back to the school used to make me feel uneasy and on edge, and I realised I still had quite a way to go on my healing journey.

There were more arrests outstanding for Mero's murder, and I received a call from Paul Davies, who was dealing with the case to say they had put out a search for Giovanni Lawrence because he was on the run, and there were still two more boys they were looking for. I felt angry but determined that the police would catch them. The press release, which showed Lawrence's face, appealed for information for his whereabouts. I posted the picture on Mero's Facebook page and asked everyone to share it, and hundreds of people did. The fourth boy Xavier Wynter still hadn't been caught, but I supposed it was only a matter of time before they all were. In the meantime, my anxiety was going through the roof. I just wanted them all caught and behind bars where they belonged, for taking the life of my angel, and where they couldn't hurt anyone else.

Nicola came over one evening and commented that I didn't have a Christmas tree up and asked if I'd like her to put it up for me. I replied that I wasn't bothered, and despite my lack of interest, she persisted. The hardest part of looking at the tree was seeing the baubles with my son's image on them, instead of him being here with me. Earlier my sister phoned and asked if Remi and I would like to spend Christmas with her, I said yes. On Christmas Eve, I spent it with Remi, Sadie, and Caerus. It was comforting that we were together, but there was still a missing piece in my heart without my Mero being with us. He loved Christmas and family time. I think that's why I struggled putting up the Christmas tree, because Mero and Remi would always help me.

The next day, Christmas Day, my first without Mero, made me feel so lost and empty inside. I cried getting dressed, but then I thought to myself; *'Come on, Kelly, you still have Remi and Caerus'*. I wiped away my tears and I watched my grandson open his presents before he left. Remi and I went to Naomi's house, where Damien, D'margio, Paige, D'neay, Mo, Chace, Deanne, D'mornae, Rohshan, Diyari, Lacey, Denny and Colleen, had all gathered. Naomi was cooking and around me the family were laughing and having fun, but I felt so lonely. I was drifting in and out of deep thoughts, and when I was asked if I was okay, I would lie and say that I was fine and try to pick myself up and join in the fun, but it was very hard. We sat down to dinner, and afterwards we played on the headset, and Errol dropped in; so did Sadie and Caerus.

I had brought fireworks, and we went to the empty carpark across from Naomi's townhouse, where Damien stood in the middle of the carpark, and we stood back and watched as he let them off. It was emotional looking up at the fireworks lighting up the dark sky, and through my tears, I shouted: 'Happy Christmas, son!' Damien's mum Colleen hugged me and asked if I was okay, I didn't reply; I could only stare at her. How could I be okay, despite being surrounded by so much love, and trying my best to enjoy myself when my baby wasn't here with me, and the crushing loneliness and emptiness I was feeling were beyond words?

Chapter Six

I always knew I wanted another child, as I didn't want Rhammel, or Remi as he's known, to be an only child. When I found out I was expecting again, I was excited but nervous, and throughout my pregnancy I constantly asked myself if I could do this, be the mother of two children. I was twenty-nine years old when I had my second child: Rhamero Latteece West. The day I went into labour I was at home with Remi, who was seven years old at the time and was playing with his toys. I was sitting on the sofa eating pineapple to try to bring on my labour because I was tired, and I now wanted him here with us. After midday the contractions started, and after a visit to the toilet, my plug fell out and I began to panic, because it was just Remi and me at home. So I phoned my mum to collect Remi, and then I phoned Naomi, who along with Errol was my birth partner, to take me to hospital.

She came and as we drove to hospital I swore at her because she was driving over the speed bumps quickly, which hurt. We picked Errol up and went to the labour ward, where they put me in a side room because I wasn't dilated fully. I was given gas and air, but it wasn't doing anything for my pain. My sister laughed at me, saying I was a wimp when it came to pain. Errol was pacing up and down the room scratching his head. After half an hour, a nurse came into the room, and I told her that I shouldn't be going through this. She asked why that was, and I told her I was supposed to be having a C-section. She checked my notes and then I was on my way to the theatre. The anaesthetist inserted a needle in my lower back to numb the pain, and then I was lying on the bed waiting for the procedure to begin, as well as for Errol, my birth partner, to arrive.

When I looked up, Naomi entered the room. I asked where Errol was and she replied he was too afraid to come into the theatre and was waiting in the side room. Naomi, dressed in a blue gown and mask, stood by my side, and I could feel the doctor putting pressure on my stomach, and I then felt relief when my baby boy was delivered. He was lifted over the curtain and we both cried when we first saw him. The nurse took him away to clean him up, and Naomi went to tell Errol that everything had gone well, and that he was the father of a baby boy weighing seven pounds and two ounces. My baby was finally brought to us in the side room, where Errol held him and announced that his name was Rhamero Latteece West. He had chosen both of the names for our boys, but didn't choose to tell me. He came up with the name because the beginning 'Rham', was half of his brother's name Rhammel, and then 'ero' was from Errol. Latteece was made up of Latifah and Cloreece, who are his cousins.

Seeing Mero for the first time, I was filled with so much joy and love, and gratitude to be blessed with another son. I felt nothing but unconditional love. There is no other love quite like it. Rhamero was so pale, and he had a full head of straight jet-black hair, and the one thing that stood out for me was his nose. He had his dad's big nose, and in fact he was the image of his dad, but just pale. Looking at his fingertips, I could see that over time, his colour would get darker. With having a C-section, I had to stay in hospital for a couple of days. I could barely move and the nurses looked after Rhamero so I could sleep.

The next morning, I got out of bed and had a shower. I was in so much pain I was bent double, afraid to straighten because it put too much pressure on my stomach. After my shower the nurse brought Rhamero into me and helped me wash and dress him and then left us alone. I remember looking down at him, thinking, W*ow, you are mine*. Errol and family came to see me, and everyone noticed that Rhamero had Errol's nose. Shaun and my sister visited, bringing with them clothes for Rhamero, and when they were getting ready to leave, my hormones kicked in and I cried because at that point I wanted to go home with Rhamero.

A few days later after final checks on both me and Rhamero, we were allowed to go home. Errol and Remi came to collect us. Rhamero and I sat in the back of the car, with the blue baby boy balloons hanging out of the windows. As we pulled up outside my flat, Errol beeped his horn to signify our return. Remi was besotted with his baby brother; he kept staring at him and always wanted to help him. He liked feeding Rhamero with me. I was so happy to be at home together with my boys. Bringing up two children wasn't as hard as I thought it was going to be, plus I had help from Errol. I was living in a two bedroom flat at the time and I wanted more space, because Mero was sleeping in my bedroom, while Remi had his own. I spoke to a neighbour, and she said that she wanted to exchange her three bedroomed house for my flat. I got in touch with my housing office and the local councillor and my exchange was granted. I was ecstatic. I now had my first ever family house, and it was two seconds away from my flat, and we did loads of car journeys to move my stuff. I didn't have much given that we were living in a flat. I was excited that the boys had their own rooms, and Bucklow Avenue with its big gardens and great neighbours was a perfect place to bring up my boys.

Now, I consider myself to be a normal woman, who worked at Wilbraham Primary School. I'd worked there for over fifteen years as a teaching assistant. Towards the end of my time there, I became an after-school club manager, working each day from eight thirty to five thirty. I loved working with children; it was all I'd ever wanted to do since leaving Shena Simon College, where I studied childcare. I worked with children who were four and five years old, which is reception age. I loved going to work, because every day was different and if I had a bad day, the children would never fail to brighten up my mood. My colleagues weren't just work colleagues; they were like my second family. The laughs we had on a daily basis were what got us through the days. The one thing I hated was being cold, and having to be outdoors on playground duty was my kind of hell. We had to do playground duty every day. I didn't mind in the summer, but in winter I would have a hot water bottle on my stomach to keep me warm. My colleagues used to laugh at me, because even in the classroom I brought my own heater from home, and I was the first to turn up the heating as soon as I got into work.

The staff at Wilbraham knew how good I was when it came to drawing, painting, and anything creative. On one occasion the head master, Steve, approached me and asked if I could turn a spare room in the school into a library area, in the shape of a castle. I said yes and was given free time to do it. I painted the castle walls and windows, drawing ivy down the walls to give an authentic effect. On another occasion I painted pictures on the walls outside the reception area. These walls were dull and needed brightening up. Depending on the characters in the books the children read I used to draw the characters, from the Gruffalo to Elmer. I was the first person the teachers would ask to do the displays in school, and every Christmas I would draw and paint the backdrop for the nativity plays. Over time I developed tennis elbow, which I was told was due to the painting I did. I also brought my creative side out at home. Every year I would change and decorate the boys' bedrooms to which theme they wanted. This ranged from jungle rooms, with all the animals, to Ben 10 and all of the super-heroes. I am so relaxed when I'm painting. It's sad because I can't find the time to do as much as I would like to.

I was with Errol, the father of my two boys for twenty-six years. We met when we were sixteen years old at a youth club in Hulme called Proctors. I went there with my cousin Claire and my friend Rachel. We were upstairs in the music room having a dance, but I wanted to go downstairs, and it was there I met Errol, who was standing on the stairs. He took one look at me and told me I was going to be his woman, but in my head I was thinking No. I kept seeing him around, and one evening he came to my sister, Marie's flat with his friend Eugene, who was seeing Marie. He asked me to sit in his car, and it was while we were chatting, he asked me out. I said yes and we kissed, and that's where it all began. Errol's mum Eldora treated me like her own daughter. Our bond was beautiful. I had so much respect for her, and she taught me a lot of things, cooking being one of them. Eldora also loved me, as I believed a mother should love her child, love I never received from my own mother when I was growing up.

My parents, Allan and Teresa were married but split when I was young. I have three other siblings; Allan, Naomi, and Marie, who was my eldest sister, and who sadly passed away. This was the first close death in our family and it hit us hard. Marie passed on 18 February 2014, and left behind two daughters: D'mornae and Deanne, who are now mothers themselves, D'mornae has a daughter called Daia and Deanne has a son called Diyari. My little sister Naomi has three children: D'margio, D'neay and Chace. D'neay has a son called Reign, and my brother Allan has three children with two different women, D'michie has a daughter called Darcie, another daughter called Baily, and a son called Leighton.

The relationship I had with both my parents wasn't good. My dad, who I call a sperm donor, and who was seeing two different women while married to my mum, was never there for me. Growing up all I can remember is he loved my sister Marie more because she was the first girl and my brother Allan because he was the only boy and the youngest child. My baby sister, Naomi, had a different father to us, and in fact Naomi's dad was my dad's brother. When I was little, I have memories of always being with my granddad. I felt that I wasn't wanted, and when I grew up I learned to become self-reliant, to do things for myself. My mum would always help my brother and sisters, but never me, and once when I asked her why this was, her response was that she didn't have to worry about me because I was independent. I replied that even if this was the case, it still would be nice for her to ask if she could help from time to time, which she never did, leading me to feel rejected by both of my parents.

I was a quiet girl when I was younger. Earlier on I had learned to keep how I was feeling inside. I didn't know how to express myself, to express the emotions and feelings swirling around inside me. When situations arose, where I didn't know how to cope, my way was to hold it all in and get on with life. When the affair between my mum and my dad's brother came to light, it didn't really affect me at all. Paul, my dad's brother, was the first person in my life to care for me and treat me like a daughter. I grew up calling Paul Dad, which Marie and Allan objected to, because he was our uncle, but to me he was my dad. He shaped me into the woman I am today; he guided me in my formative years, even teaching me how to how to be practical and to build stuff. Seeing my mum with different partners growing up soured my perception of relationships in a way. I used to think this type of behaviour was not great role model behaviour, and one thing I took from it was, whenever I had kids of my own, they would only have their father in their lives, and not witness the negative behaviours my mum exhibited when I was growing up, and more importantly, never suffer the same fate that I had experienced.

In the beginning, Errol and I had a good relationship, then over time it began to wear me down. I could never find the right words I wanted to say. I never felt that I was being my authentic self. I was a partner and a mother, but not Kelly Brown. I would hold a lot in and plod along with the relationship. I could never speak to Errol the way I could with other people, but at the same time I wasn't confident speaking in front of people at work, in assemblies, or in staff meetings. In 2018 our relationship broke down. I packed his stuff and told him to collect it when he finished work. At the time he was working as a personal trainer at a gym in the city centre, and then that was it, the end of twenty six years. I struggled for the first year. I felt sick and lost.

Errol was the only man I'd known since the age of sixteen. I would tell the boys I was sick and stay off work, and during the low times, I kept telling myself there was light at the end of the dark tunnel. However, it was still hard to bring up two boys alone, but I did the best for them. I'm now a nana to a beautiful grandson, Caerus, who came at the right time in my life. He is such a character and puts a smile on my face. I must say a nana's love is different from the love I feel for my sons, and he gets away with too much. Being autistic, Caerus's behaviour can be challenging at times, but the more I learn to understand him, the stronger our relationship grows. My hobbies are gardening, going to the gym, and I love spending time in nature, where I feel at peace. I enjoy meeting up with friends and having fun. My dreams are to be working for myself, living a stress-free life, and travelling the world.

Chapter Seven

The New Year began, and I was still left with an empty heart. Then the news we were all waiting for came in, the news that they had caught Giovanni Lawrence at a Travel Lodge in Cheshire, and by luck they caught Xavier Wynter in a stolen car. Both were in custody and now there was a wait for the CPS to give the go ahead to charge them with murder. The wait for the phone call was a long one, and my heart beat anxiously in my chest. After a few hours, Paul finally called back with the news that the CPS had agreed to charge all four with murder. I didn't know how to feel. I was experiencing such a range and mixture of emotions all at once. I was angry that they had done this, but empty because part of me had died with Mero. The whole process had destroyed me inside, but I knew I had to fight this for my baby boy.

The love I felt in Fallowfield was beautiful, but I needed to move to a new area, with new faces and where no one knew us. My request for a house swap came through, and I felt sad because I would never have left my house because I loved it, and had it looking as I wanted it, both inside and out. However, since Mero's death I knew I couldn't stay there any longer. I was struggling with simple things, like going to the shops, where people stared at me wondering if I was okay, and worse, seeing Mero's friends, thinking he should be with them. In mid-January, two removal vans turned up outside the house and friends and family came and helped pack up the house. Sadness came over me, as the reality of leaving the house I thought I'd grow old in sank in. I was also sad to leave my neighbours, who in the fifteen years I had lived there had been so supportive. It was especially hard to say goodbye to Dave and Debbie who lived across the way. Dave had a heart of gold and was like a father, always doing odd jobs for me. I'll never forget when I first moved into Bucklow Avenue, he made me a wishing well and a bench for my back garden. But I knew that I would still keep in touch no matter where I went.

Thankfully the day was dry and once the house had been emptied it was time for me to say goodbye to this chapter of my life. Remi and I walked around the house taking it all in for the last time, and as I stood in Mero's room, I took a deep breath, looked around, and then walked out. We all got into our cars and drove in a convoy to the new house. We were met by Gaynor and Cloreece, and other family and friends. However, we couldn't move in just yet because the family who lived in the house were still packing up, so we piled my belongings in the front garden. After waiting for a little while we were able to move in. I was overwhelmed with it all. My cousin kept on reassuring me that it would all work out, and that they were all here to help. Then it hit me again; I had moved with only one child. Holding back my tears, I just got on with it and moved into another three-bedroomed house, so I could have a bedroom for Mero's stuff. Cloreece, and Claire, worked into the early hours trying to make it comfortable for us both, and at some point, Remi and I fell into bed exhausted.

Waking up in a new house felt weird knowing Mero wasn't with us. The house was quiet, and I thought this shouldn't be happening, but I knew I had to accept that it was. Family and friends helped me to paint and to make the house feel like a home. Mero's dad, Errol, painted Mero's room all white for me. He spent most of the day painting. It was hard for him and he cried, but he didn't stop until he'd finished. Once the paint was dry, I went into the room and made-up Mero's bed and unpacked his things like he was still here. I couldn't let go of anything. I put his computer on his desk and his TV at the bottom of his bed. On the shelves above his bed I put all the remarkable things people have brought me for Mero. I hung the flag that had photos of Mero on it on the large wall of the bedroom. It brought comfort to me to kiss the photos when I came into his room, or walked past it. Originally, I wanted it to be my grandson, Caerus's room too, but I couldn't bring myself to allow him, or anyone else to go in there. It was Mero's room and that was that. Over the weeks, Caerus kept going in and touching Mero's things. He was only three years old, but I found myself getting upset and annoyed. I understood he just wanted to look and touch, but in the end and for my own peace of mind, I brought a lock and key, and kept the door locked so no one could go into his room when I wasn't there.

My home eventually started to feel like our home, and I was staying in quite a lot, when one day my friend Neffie invited me round to her house for dinner. This day was different because all I kept thinking was that I wanted to share my story. I was ready to speak about it publicly from the day I lost Mero. I drove to

Neffie's and spent the day chilling with her and her two daughters Nubia and Tari. It was nice to get out of the house for a while, but I didn't say anything about what I wanted to do, I kept it to myself. When I got home and was getting ready for bed, I sat down, positioned my phone on the drawers, took a deep breath and pressed record. My heart was beating quickly, and I was nervous and anxious, but I knew it was something I wanted to do, I *had* to do. I spoke about the events of that day and how I felt about it, and how it had changed my life forever. I cried as I spoke and for the first time I was showing thousands of people the real me, which was something I had never done before. I usually held my tears in or cried behind closed doors. I wanted to get across that it was okay to open up and cry and allow feelings to flow, and not to worry who was watching. When I finished, I pressed the stop button and wiped away my tears. I posted the video on Mero's Facebook page; despite feeling nervous about putting it out there, I wanted to share what I was going through, to share the pain that losing Mero had created. For me that video was one of my biggest achievements. I had finally learned to open up. After minutes of the video being posted, I was receiving text and Facebook messages from friends and followers sending me love and support, saying that it was the first time they had heard what had happened and what I was going through, and how brave I was to share my experience with them.

A week later I contacted the Violence Reduction Unit again and asked for another meeting. I went with my niece Deanne, and we met with Damian Dallimore, the director of the unit. I told him that as a mother who had lost her child to knife crime, my voice needed to be heard, and I showed the video I'd recorded for Facebook. He was touched and after the meeting with Damian I was asked to contribute to a video that was being recorded to support a knife crime campaign, whose strap line was: 'Speaking out could save a life.' I agreed and on the day of filming, which was held in a youth hub, I was shown into a small room. Inside, there were two men who were filming. I was guided on what to say. 'My name is Kelly Brown and I'm from Manchester. My son Mero West was killed last September in 2021, due to being a victim of knife crime. The impact of knife crime has destroyed me. Part of me died on the day my son was killed. People who carry knives really need to think about the consequences of their actions, for the victim's life, as well as their own lives, the family's lives and for the community. They need to reach out to someone if they're worried about themselves, or someone else. Just reach out and speak to someone because there is help out there. Speaking out could save a life.' Afterwards, I was excited, and was told I would receive a link when it had been edited and produced.

Shortly after this I was approached by Jacqui Carroll, who ran Reel MCR with her partner Terry, and who was putting together a short documentary on knife crime, which was called 'No Safe Place'. Jacqui wanted to get my message out and asked me to share my story after she had watched the post I had shared on Facebook. I said yes straight-away, because I knew it was important to get my message across on the effects of knife crime mothers and families are left to deal with. We arranged a date, and I went to their studio, which was based at St Wilfrid's Street in Hulme, with my niece Deanne and her son Diyari. I was wearing a purple hoodie which had 'Mero's World Foundation' printed on it. Jacqui met me and I was introduced to her husband Jamie, who also worked for Reel MCR, I was feeling both nervous and anxious when Jacqui showed me into a room where a chair was placed in the middle, with bright lights and cameras pointing to the chair. She kept reassuring me that everything would be okay. I sat down on the chair and students filmed me as Jacqui asked me questions, like: What's your name? Can you tell me what happened on 9 September? What was Mero like? At the end we hugged and she told me she would be in touch once the documentary had been completed, and as I drove home in the dark, I was happy to have been given the opportunity to add my voice to the video.

The next morning, I got up and went downstairs to make a cup of tea. I don't watch TV since Mero's death. I prefer to listen to music. Each morning, I play 'Baby Boy', which was played at Mero's funeral, and have played it every day since his passing. I then kiss one of his pictures which are in every room in the house. It gives me comfort to see his face. I received a text from Maggie; she said that she had talked to Old Trafford Council and Old Trafford Creative Space, who create all of the murals in Trafford, and they discussed the possibility of doing a mural for Mero on Norton Street. Later on I went to an open day where I met Linda from Old Trafford Creative

Space, as well as Maggie, Kate and a few of the neighbours, and we all shared our ideas on what we would like to see included in the mural. We wrote our ideas on sticky notes, and Kate wrote a purple heart, since that was Mero's favourite colour and the colour I use when I send messages, and I wrote down 'Baby Boy' in memory of the song I play each morning. Once we'd agreed on the content, Maggie pushed for the mural to be finished for 9 September, which was Mero's one-year anniversary. When I go back to Norton Street, the experience always breaks my heart, and leaves me feeling bitter sweet. I feel bitter that my son has gone, but also grateful that a beautiful mural in memory of him had been created.

Chapter Eight

I received an email from Mel from the Violence Reduction Unit. She sent me a clip of the campaign video I had contributed to. When I watched the clip, I felt it was very powerful. Mel said that they were having a press release on 11 February, and she asked if I would like to attend, where once the release had finished I could share the video on my social media platforms. I emailed her and told her I would love to take part in the press release. A week later, I went with my niece Deanne to the offices where the event was happening. Mel met us and showed us into a room where there were rows of chairs and four chairs at the front of the room. Reporters from the BBC, ITV and the *Manchester Evening News* were waiting, and I began to feel very nervous, because it all looked so professional. Mel asked me if I knew Matthew Norford, who was involved in the campaign video. I replied that I didn't and she took me over to him and introduced us. Matthew looked at me and asked how my husband was. I replied straightaway, telling him me and Errol were no longer together, and then I said hi, and at the same moment thought he was really cute.

I was then asked to go and meet Andy Burnham, who was waiting in another room. After a short while, we all went back into the main room where Bev Hughes, the deputy mayor, Matthew, chairman of 1message, Andy Burnham and I were directed to sit at the front of the room, facing the press. I remember seeing Deanne sitting in the audience and thinking if I just focus on her I will be okay. Being under the scrutiny of so many reporters made me feel nervous and out of my depth. One by one we had to introduce ourselves, as well as say a little bit about who we are. I introduced myself as Kelly Brown, the mother of Rhamero West who was stabbed and killed in Old Trafford on 9 September 2021, and also chair of the Mero's World Foundation. My anxiety levels went through the roof when I had to speak, and I just wanted it over with, but I was glad that I had taken part. It was a huge thing for me to do, as it was only months after Mero's death, and here I was speaking in front of the national news.

After the video had been aired, each of the panel had to do interviews for different reporters. I spoke to all of them about the campaign I was involved in. The last interview took place outside in the garden area, and when it ended, I went home feeling very proud of myself. On the same day as it was aired, the video went viral, and I shared it on Mero's social media platforms, and I was getting tagged in posts that people had seen showing my face promoting the campaign. My face seemed to be everywhere, and I even paid a visit to the tram stop in Chorlton to take a picture of myself in front of the bill board raising awareness of knife crime.

It had taken the ambulance thirty minutes to reach Mero, and our internet research showed that there were bleed cabinets that would help stem the victim's bleeding until the ambulance arrived. The cabinets were simple to use; all that was needed was for someone to dial 999 and the police would give a unique code to open the cabinet. Once inside there is a coded map of the body for the user to follow. The user doesn't need to be trained in first aid techniques. All they have to do is to apply the correct colour package for the corresponding area to stem the bleed until professional help arrives. We enquired about the costs of the cabinet and did a raffle on our Mero's World site and managed to raise enough money to buy a cabinet. We asked Lil, who worked in the library in Fallowfield, if they would install it there. She agreed and was very supportive, so we decided to organise an event to raise money for more cabinets.

On 12 February, we installed the first ever cabinet. It meant a lot to me because it was the first one in Mero's name and it was also my birthday. With help from Karla, Nicola, Gaynor, Jade, Deanne, Neffie, Hayley and Claire and members of the community, we managed to hold our first event. We had different stalls, food, raffles, a beer van, music, and entertainment. It was such a good day, and at one point Gillian got hold of the mic and pulled me to the middle of the floor, where everybody sang 'Happy Birthday' to me. I was embarrassed, but I was grateful for everything. We went outside and unveiled the first cabinet. First, I did a speech, thanking everyone for coming and promised that it was going to be the first of many in memory of my baby boy. Everyone clapped and congratulated me, and afterwards we went back to my house for a birthday drink, and counted the money raised, which was enough to buy another two cabinets.

The next day, reporters were ringing me asking for interviews. They wanted to do features on us because it was the first ever cabinet installed in Manchester, and my face was all over the news again. I was contacted by a man called Paddy via Facebook. He had seen me on the news with the bleed cabinets, and he was eager to have the same in Bury where he lived. Paddy, Tina, and Wendy started fund raising in Bury, and eventually we had a meeting over Zoom. He asked if I would do the education side of things, to which I agreed. As a mother, I wanted to get into primary schools and high schools, anywhere just to get my message across, and the devastating ripple effect knife crime has on families.

We continued with the monthly marches in different areas of Manchester. We marched through Fallowfield, Moss Side, Old Trafford, Stretford and Ladybarn, but it was on the Didsbury march I really found my voice. I made a connection with Carl Scott on Facebook. He lived in Essex and was raising awareness of knife crime in his area. I invited him to come on the march, and he did. We made a podcast together called: *Mero's World: A Mother's Quest*. We then took to the streets of Didsbury. We met outside Pizza Express and once we had assembled, we set off. It was a sunny day, and I was wearing a purple Mero's World t-shirt, and Carl was talking through the megaphone about the effects of knife crime. We were walking down Burton Road, and out of nowhere I took the megaphone from Carl and started to share my story of being a grieving mum and the impact it has on those left behind. People started coming out of shops and listening to what I had to say. My friend Neffie was walking behind me in tears. She said: 'Kelly, you have found your voice.'

On another march through Chorlton, it was wet and cold, but we didn't let that stop us from marching. Jacqui from Reel MCR came to film us and Kelly Foran from the BBC also filmed us on the march. She also interviewed my cousins Sheree and Toni and a few others to get their insight on how they had been affected by Mero's death. One of my nephews, Chace, had to receive counselling because he didn't want to go to school. He was afraid of leaving his mum and dad. He and Mero were close because Mero was always at my sister's house; it was his second home. My niece's son Diyari was scared and would ask if Auntie Kelly was going to die. Diyari was also like a little brother to Mero. He always took time out to go to see Diyari, and it was heart-breaking to see the result Mero's death had on the younger members of the family.

During one of the marches, I met a mum called Joanie Dixon. She had lost her own son Kennie Carter to knife crime when he was also sixteen. We chatted and the result was to have a march together through the Stretford area. This was a strong and powerful march of two grieving mothers, fighting for a change against knife crime. Joanie and I were at the head of the procession, and when I turned, all I could see was a sea of purple and yellow t-shirts, people holding banners and chanting 'Stop knife crime'. Jacqui filmed the march for her documentary, and we both did interviews for the local radio reporters. At the end of the march, the bleed cabinet was installed in Kennie's memory and with a picture of him and Mero on it outside the Bargain Booze shop. Joanie gave a speech for the boys and we went back to her house, where we gave another interview, in which we talked about the loss of our boys and coming together to tackle knife crime.

Chapter Nine

The weekend before the court case, I was feeling nervous, sickly, and overwhelmed, but knew that I was finally going to face the boys who took my baby's life. The date for the trial was coming up, and Louise from Victim Support contacted me, asking if they could help with our travelling costs, as it was going to be a six-week trial. I spoke to Louise and told her I would be doing the driving, and the family would be coming with me. She told me to keep all my parking receipts so I would be reimbursed at the end of the trial, and she also told me to stay strong, and that she was here for me. I thanked her, and admitted that I was scared, but had my family supporting me.

On 7 March 2022, I woke up around 7:00am because we had to be at court before 9:00am. I dressed in black pants, a shirt and a smart black coat. Tracey, the liaison officer arrived at my house, and she drove me and my sister to court, I was going to meet my two nieces Deanne and D'mornae, as well as Errol, there. My heart was racing as we arrived at the front doors of the court. Inside, we were searched by security and then were directed to Court Room 3. There were police officers everywhere. Next to the court room was a side room. Inside, I was met by two barristers, a man and a woman who were fighting for justice for Mero, and they both assured me that they would do their very best throughout the court case.

When the families of the boys started to come in, I felt angry seeing them, Keliah, the mother of Marquis and her dad were sitting down and as I went to take a seat. She looked at me and then they both got up and walked away, but I did my best to remain strong. As I looked around the hallway, the atmosphere felt cold and empty. Tracey explained that nothing much was going to happen today because it was the start of it all. When we were given the signal to enter the court, we were guided to sit at the bottom. To our left was the glass box where the boys would be seated. Their families were seated upstairs, away from me and my family. We were informed that we would be able to enter the court by the back entrance and have the use of the family room before court began and during the break times.

My sister held one of my hands and my niece D'mornae held the other. My heart was beating so fast I was sure everyone could hear it. The boys were led up from the cells and entered the court. I stared at them, one by one. I couldn't take my eyes off them. To think these four individuals took the life of my baby. I looked at Errol, he looked at me and then looked away, and he then whispered: 'I can't do this, Kelly.' I knew he had just as much anger and hatred as I did for these boys. Looking at them was hard, and the knowledge that we were going to have to be in the same room for the next six weeks was soul destroying. But I was going to be there. Nothing was going to stop me being there every single day to look at the faces of the boys that had done this terrible thing. When the judge entered, we all stood and then sat down once he did. The first day consisted of mainly legal stuff between the barristers. We had a break, and we headed to the family room. As we walked past them, the boys' families tried to intimidate us, and the boys themselves were disrespectful, giggling and smirking and showing no remorse for what they had done. It didn't work. I held my head up high and stared at them all. Inside, I vowed: you have taken my son, but you will *never* see me break.

The family room was warm and comfortable. We had the use of a TV, fridge, kettle, and we had a cup of tea before the afternoon session. Errol left; he couldn't handle the fact of seeing the boys, and I understood how hard it was for him, as a man and the father of Rhamero. In the afternoon we were sitting in the same places as before, but there were reporters in the seats in front of us. Before the session started, I looked around the inside of the court room. The walls were wooden panelled, the seats were hard and the lighting was bright. I sat there thinking to myself. *Am I really doing this, trying to fight for justice for my son?*

When the afternoon session had ended, we were given the option of going out the back entrance, but I looked at my sister and said: 'We're walking out the front doors with everyone else.' There was no way I was hiding from anyone. As we were making our way out, the defendants' families were standing at the entrance. We walked past them and to the waiting car of my sister's boyfriend. They took me home and once inside I cried. I asked myself if I could do this, seeing those evil boys every day for the next six weeks. After a good cry, I told myself that I could do it. It was like Mero was with me, giving me the strength to go through with it. That night I had dinner with Remi and then had an early night, knowing what was ahead of me. The next day driving to court, I was more than ready to fight for Mero.

We all would meet in the family room, where we brought food supplies to last all day, so we didn't have to leave the court. On one particular day as we left the family room to go to the court room, we bumped into the judge, who was coming out of his chambers. He looked at us and smiled, and he said: 'I will do my very best to get you justice.' We all thanked him, and once in the court room we headed to our usual places, this time wrapped in thick coats as it was so cold. The family of the defendants came into the top gallery. They made so much noise, joking and laughing, and worse still when the boys were led in, they showed no remorse, they smirked and giggled up to their families, like to them it was all a game.

This particular day was different; I got to hear Mero's final movements on that day. The jury came in and after they were seated, they were each handed a folder with all the evidence the police had collected from before and after Mero had been killed. It started off with the witnesses, who were on Princess Road on 9 September, and who had filmed the incident. The witnesses gave their evidence behind a screen to protect their identities. One witness said he was standing still in traffic and told his son to record what was happening. They witnessed Marquis and Ryan getting out of their car, running up to the car Mero was in and hitting the window with a knife.

A witness, who was parked at the side of the car Mero was in, said Mero looked scared. Another witness in a Tesla said: 'I heard all the commotion and pressed record straightaway.' His car recorded ten minutes of strong evidence which was clearly of Marquis and Ryan, showing them running with a knife. From Princess Road to Chorlton Road, the defendants, like a pack of wolves chased the car Mero and his friends were in. There was so much footage of Mero running away, trying to get away after their car had crashed into a tree, and he was later seen desperately knocking on doors for help. The footage of the moment Marquis gave the knife to Ryan was also caught on camera, and when he caught up to Mero he said: 'Arrrah, I've got you now!'

Another key witness was shouting from her bedroom window for Ryan to leave Mero alone, but he stabbed Mero and then got into the car and drove away. The witness said she shouted for Mero to cross the road and to walk to her. It must have been the adrenaline rushing through his body for him to be able to stand up and go to the woman, where he then collapsed on her doorstep. At this point other neighbours came out to help, trying to stem the bleeding. There was also footage that had been recorded of just the sound of Mero shouting to his friends, but before this was played the judge asked me if I wanted to leave the court or stay. I told him I was okay, and I wanted to stay. They played the footage and I could hear Mero shouting for his friends. Inside this was breaking me, as I could hear the fear in his voice, signalling that he had been hurt. While it was playing I just looked down at the floor until the recording stopped. I took a deep breath and looked up again.

In court, the barrister made us aware of the high number of calls from concerned members of the public to the emergency services on that day. In all there were six key witnesses, who came forward, and all I could keep thinking was; *Thank goodness these people came forward*, and I was grateful it would help catch the boys who did this to Mero. After listening to all the evidence put forward that day I was drained mentally and physically. Having to grieve the loss of my child as well as listen to his last moments played in court, hearing him shouting, sounding so scared, was destroying. On the journey home from court, I screamed and cried, and when Errol phoned me, I couldn't speak. He told me he was coming over, and when he arrived at my house, I went straight into his arms and cried, and he didn't leave until he knew I was okay.

Every day in court, even though I was surrounded and supported by friends and family, I felt lost with it all. I didn't know whether I was coming or going. Now it was time for the defendants to give their evidence, Ryan went into the witness box and said he wasn't at the scene where Mero was stabbed. He told the jury he got out of the car when they were on Princess Road, where the chase started. Our barrister asked why his phone was tracked from GPS, which showed he was at the scene. He went on to say he had left his phone in the car and had run off from Princess Road. After he had been questioned he returned to the glass dock. When it was Giovanni's turn for questioning, he claimed he had sold his phone on the day of the murder, and he too was never there, despite the fact that his phone was tracked all day and the boys were all together and more importantly his DNA was found on the door of the stolen car. Giovanni even produced a witness claiming to have bought the phone from him.

It was all becoming too much, but I was holding it together, and the lunch break came at the right time. The four defendants were escorted back to the cells, their families left the gallery, and we were escorted to the family room to have lunch. Before I knew it, the hour was up, and we were back in court. It was time for Marquis to go into the witness box. He said he was there, but he didn't know Mero, he just wanted to scare him, but he did more than that. Xavier was the only defendant who didn't want to go into the witness box to give evidence. Doing the same routine of listening to their lies was wearing away at my soul, and I worried that the jury was going to actually believe the lies they were saying. The time came for them to present their alibis; back and forth it went. Keliah, Marquis's mum, gave the police the track suit he was wearing on that day when they went to her house. It had been washed and was drying on a radiator.

Ryan's barrister claimed he wasn't there, and it wasn't him on the footage, but one police officer said he was 99 per cent certain that it was Ryan Cashin, as he had distinct cheek bones. Ryan was also wearing a black hoodie, and his barrister was going round in circles, saying Ryan was wearing a blue hoodie, and even made a mockery of the police, saying they had got the colour wrong. He even brought one to court to try to trick the police officer, and to talk about irrelevant things to confuse the jury, but the judge took the hoodie away and told the barrister to ask only appropriate questions, and for the jury to ignore what they had just seen.

During the break, my cousin, Toni, told me that she saw Marquis's dad, Junior, a few times and that he had tried to intimidate her. I was angry. I told her I wasn't scared of him, and when I saw him, I was going to have something to say. I got my chance when I came out of the toilet. Junior was sitting outside the court. I walked over and asked him why he was intimidating my cousin. He denied it, and at that exact moment Toni walked past us. He stared at her and then looked at me and said he was pissed off and didn't mean it. I told him I wasn't threatened by him. My son's life was taken and I would be fighting this all the way to the end. He didn't say anything in reply; he just stared at me, as I got up and walked back into the court room.

A police officer who specialised in tracking the GPS signals from mobile phones told the jury the whereabouts of the boys from that morning all the way until they had chased Mero. The evidence was right there for the jury to see, but I was still afraid and doubting that the boys would be found not guilty and would get away with killing my son. The judge dismissed the court at four o'clock, because he had heard enough for the day, and told us the court would be sitting again at nine o'clock the next day. Going home, I was feeling in a daze with it all, trying to take it all in. Reliving it was one of the hardest things I've ever had to do; the first was losing Mero. I didn't realise how painful it would be, holding back the tears, refusing to let any of them see me crumble.

It was the day when the defendants' barristers were reading out their closing speech after our barrister had done theirs. I was afraid and asked Paul why they did it that way. I was concerned the jury would forget everything and get side-tracked with what the defendant's barristers would say. Paul reassured me and said it was just the procedure, and that it would be fine. When we entered court, we were asked to sit on the back row, which was the row behind where we usually sat. I questioned this and was told the defendants' families and friends up in the gallery have bottles of water and they didn't want us to be a target. I later found out they had been taking pictures from the gallery in court, and now they had to hand in their phones, so they couldn't do it. One of their friends even got removed from court because he refused to hand his phone in, and he wasn't allowed back in court. Ryan's barrister stood up and in his closing, speech went off track and started talking about being on holiday. I really wasn't sure what he was trying to do. The rest of the barristers kept their closing speeches short.

The judge addressed the jury and said under the Joint Enterprise Law they could find the boys guilty of murder, manslaughter, or not guilty. The jury stood up and filed out of the court room, taking their folders with them. Having to sit through and listen to six weeks of evidence, reliving my baby's last moments, was torture. As I said before, going to court was one of the hardest things I've done in my life, and I was scared that the jury held justice for him in their hands. We were told to go to the family room and wait. We had to play the waiting game, waiting for the jury to come back with their verdict. The only verdict I wanted to hear was that they found the boys guilty of Mero's murder; however, by four o'clock, they hadn't returned, so we were sent home.

I went to the cemetery to see Mero, it was raining and cold, so I didn't stay long. I stood beside his grave looking at his picture. I couldn't sit on the bench because it was too wet. After ten minutes I left. Grief comes in waves, and you never know when it will hit you. I cry at night when Remi is staying at his girlfriend's house, its then I can really let all my pain out, where I cry and scream into my pillow. When I got into my car, I burst into tears, crying so hard I had to pull over, and for an hour I cried, screamed, and hit the steering wheel. When the tears stopped, I wiped my eyes, and came to the unbearable acceptance that I was going to have this for the rest of my life.

The next day, we went into the court by the back entrance and had to wait in the family room until the jury returned. My heart was racing and my anxiety levels were high. I couldn't eat. All I wanted to know was that all of the boys would be convicted of murder. I sat on the sofa and in my head I was asking Mero for a sign. I suddenly looked at my sister and asked her if she felt what I had just felt. She replied: 'Do you mean the cold feeling?' I smiled and nodded. I felt a cold feeling touching my hand. It was like Mero was holding my hand, the first ever time I felt him.

We were called back to court as the jury had now returned. My heart was racing as we were escorted to the court room. We had to enter by a different door, as the families of the defendants were being loud and making a fuss. Liz, Paul, and Tracey were all sitting in the court room. There were also reporters wanting to speak with me, but I didn't want to speak to any of them, I just wanted justice for my boy. The four defendants came up from the cells, and the jury came in. When the judge appeared, we stood, and then we were seated. He asked the jury if they had come to a decision, and they replied that they had for one of the defendants. My sister held my hand tightly as they said they found the defendant Ryan Cashin guilty of murdering Rhamero West. I gave a loud sigh, and my sister started to cry. Ryan was then removed from the court and taken down to the cells. The judge then released the jury to make a decision on the other three defendants.

We were sent to the family room, where I had a cry with the girls. Nothing else happened that day, so we were sent home. I tried to tell Remi, but like his dad Errol, he didn't want to know anything until they were all convicted. We went back and forth that week, the jury not deciding on the rest of them, and it was killing me having to sit every day in the family room, praying the jury would do the right thing. On the Thursday, we were called into court. The jury wanted to ask the judge a question about the case. The judge told them if they couldn't come to a decision, it would have to go to deadlock. I didn't understand this and when the judge released the jury again, I asked Paul what it meant. He replied that it would have to go to a retrial, and I thought that there was no way I wanted to go through all of that again. Back in the family room I told the girls I didn't want it to go to deadlock, and they told me I had to stay positive.

Friday came and we went back to court. My sister, my nieces and my friends Paula and Karla were also there. Once again, we were waiting in the family room. The atmosphere was quieter. We just wanted the jury to come back with their verdict. Halfway through the morning we were called to court. As we walked back to court, my legs were like jelly, because I knew that this was it. Reporters and the police were in court, Tracey, Liz, and Paul were there sitting in front of us, and they asked if I was okay. I nodded my head and smiled. The defendants, Giovanni, Xavier and Marquis were led into court. The judge asked the jury if they had reached a verdict, to which they replied they had. My heart was beating so loud, and I held on to my sister's hand, and the foreman of the jury spoke. They said they found Marquis Richards and Giovanni Lawrence guilty of murder and Xavier Wynter not guilty. The noise from the defendant's families was so loud, they were clearly unhappy with the verdict. The judge had to tell them to be quiet, and as Marquis was being led down to the cells, he turned and looked at us and did a cut-throat gesture, and said: 'Mero got smoked.' We remained calm and stayed in the court room until it was empty.

Throughout the case these four individuals showed absolutely no remorse for their actions, or respect for us, Mero's grieving family. The judge announced that sentencing would take place in May. I hugged Liz, Paul and Tracey and went home, where I phoned Errol to let him know what happened. I also told Remi, and that evening we spent absorbing it all. It was almost over; the fight was coming to an end.

Chapter Ten

Waking up the next morning, I lay in bed and was thinking it was all over, now the court case had finished. Things were getting back to normal - well, my normal is totally different now. For months I'd been running off adrenaline, but now I thought it was time I grieved for the loss of my child without thinking about anything else. There were many days when I would feel so lost, numb and empty inside, desperate for a sign from Mero for some comfort. Most evenings I would sit on my bed with the television on in the background and be on my phone. One particular evening when I was in my room, I felt a soft touch against my forehead, and I knew this was Mero. It happens when I am deep in thought and ask him to give me a sign.

I can wake up one day and feel fine, but all it takes is to see something that reminds me of Mero, and then I feel down, in a low mood that I cannot snap out of, just wanting to cry and scream. I have come to learn that the kind of grief that involves losing a child is like being on a roller coaster; it comes in waves, and you never know what you're going to feel from one moment to the next. I've lost family members before, and even my beloved sister, Marie; however, the loss of a child is so painful, like your heart has been ripped out. I don't have many people to talk to, and I have kept a lot inside. This is because for most of my life I've had to deal with any problems I have faced by myself.

Each morning since Mero was taken, I get up and the first thing I have to do is turn on YouTube and play the song 'Baby Boy'. I go to the cemetery once a week to make sure his resting place is clean and tidy and to bring a purple rose for him. I am a deeply spiritual person, and I know Mero's spirit has left his body and is finally free. I also know he isn't there; it's just the shell of his body. I don't need to go to the cemetery to talk to him; I do that at home, or anywhere I am. One positive thing I can take from losing my son, is that now I have the best guiding angel walking beside me every day.

To try to get some normality back into my life, I went back to work. I had a meeting with the headmaster, Steve, and he arranged phased returns. I started off doing mornings, and then afternoons. Nothing class based, just doing jobs around the school. It was hard coming back into Fallowfield to work, walking past the astro pitch where Mero used to hang out and play football, and having the visions of him riding up on his bright orange bike to come and see me at work were hard. On the other hand, it did help me get back into a routine, and to face life head on. The days and weeks went by and I was feeling okayish. Towards the end of the school year, I put in a transfer request to be moved out of Reception and to be moved to Year One. I felt I needed a change and that I would challenge myself and learn new skills, because I had worked in Reception for over fifteen years. I had a meeting with the head master, the two deputy heads Andy, and Sarah, where I addressed how I was feeling. They said they would see what they could do. I also talked to my manager, Jacqui, and told her how I felt.

Before the end of the school year, I learned that I was staying in Reception when school started in September. I felt disappointed, as well as disheartened, because it felt like no one was listening to me and how I was feeling and what I wanted. If I'm honest this was the final straw that caused me to leave Wilbraham Primary School, because it seemed they didn't have my best interests at heart, and I was also concerned about my mental health. I needed the challenge of embarking on a new routine, rather than doing the same thing, and I realised I was over-thinking things, and I decided in September I was going to give it a chance to see how things panned out. But during the first week of the holidays, I woke up one morning and emailed my resignation to all of the managers. As soon as I sent it, it felt like a weight had been lifted from my shoulders. It was a scary decision that I had to make at the time, but the best decision I had made in a long time.

After our first event in February I decided that I wanted to set up a foundation for Mero, I came up with the name Mero's World Foundation. I knew it was time to focus and to put all my energy into Mero's Foundation, as at the time we were only focussing on installing the bleed cabinets. I started looking after Karla's grandparents, Rose, and Peter, in the morning, which was giving me the rest of the day to work on the Foundation. I thought long and hard on who I was going to ask to come on board with me. I knew I wanted to bring together a network of strong women, because that's who had got me through everything that had happened so far in my journey. All the women I chose have different strengths and qualities; Jade is a councillor, Gaynor works in mental health, Deanne is studying Criminology and Psychology. Neffie is a primary school teacher, and Hayley is a deputy head in a primary school. I am a mother who has experienced losing a child, first-hand. They all were happy to be a part of the Foundation when I approached them, and over one evening Hayley and I worked together filling out the forms with as much detail as we could. At one point, I looked at Hayley, and asked if she would like to be part of the team, and she replied that I hadn't needed to ask her, as she wanted to help anyway. I insisted that I wanted her to come on board, and she smiled and thanked me.

Hayley completed the forms, which I couldn't thank her enough for. Back and forth she went liaising with the Charity Commission. They sent the forms back because of missing information. We were finally accepted and became a registered charity (Charity no: 1199890) in memory of my beloved son: Rhamero Latteece West. When we received the email informing us that Mero's World Foundation was now registered, I felt saddened, but excited, and happy all at once. Saddened that I'd lost my son, but excited to know I had five strong women on board, who were going to help the charity go from strength to strength. That evening we got together to celebrate at Jasmines in Chorlton, where we had food and drinks, and the first photograph of us, the trustees, was taken together. I was very grateful for Hayley's work. She fought so hard to get us registered. It was then my job to set up a bank account for our charity. It turned out to be a long process, as the bank didn't just need my details, but the details of the rest of the board. It took two months for everything to be settled, but when it was, there was no holding us back from moving forward as a charity. The trustees of the Foundation are Deanne Brown, Deanne Lee, Hayley Wright, Gaynor Holden, and Jade Doswell, and with the help from two volunteers, Natasha, and her daughter Mia, we came together and decided to open a youth hub. I also wanted to give back to Fallowfield, the area Mero loved, and to install bleed cabinets around Greater Manchester.

We ran the youth hub every Friday from 5:30pm to 7:30pm from the library. It was both challenging and rewarding, to provide a safe place for the children to attend. We provided food and drinks and different activities; that included team building, boxing, and more importantly, allowing them to be kids. On one occasion we took fifteen kids bowling, it was hard, and I questioned if I really could do this. The children were so happy, and yes they tested the boundaries, but deep down I knew they were good kids, and I was in it for the long haul, especially when two of the kids said they had never been bowling. The youth hub grew from strength to strength with up to twenty kids attending each week.

Summer was here and we held a massive summer fair at the library to raise more money for the bleed safety cabinets. There were stalls selling food and drinks, different game stalls and bouncy castles. It was a hot day and there was an excellent turnout. From this, we had another event at the Morrisons store in Chorlton, and at the Limelight Centre in Old Trafford. On all of these occasions we received support from the local councillors and MPs. In the blink of an eye, my whole life had changed. I was now having meetings with important people, always to be followed by news reporters, having afternoon tea with the Lord Mayor of Manchester, giving interviews on knife crime, going to schools to raise awareness, and talking about the ripple effects it has on the family left behind, and supporting other mothers who had gone through the same loss I have suffered.

I had an approach via Facebook from a man called Colin who was doing a documentary which was called *Knife Crime*, and I agreed to be part of it by sharing my story. I went to his house where I met his wife, and the filming took place in the living room and afterwards when I was looking at pictures of Mero, I felt like finally, my voice was being heard. I then did two pieces for the BBC, one with Mike Sweeney in my home with my niece Deanne, where I talked about the day I lost Mero, and installing the bleed cabinets across Greater Manchester. The other was with Alex Beresford called *Stop and Search*. It seemed to me, every time something was happening regarding knife crime in Manchester, I would be contacted by the press to give my views on the subject.

Mero and me eight weeks old

Four months old

Age Six

Age Seven

Age Nine

Age Fourteen

Age Fifteen

Age Sixteen

Chapter Eleven

A few days after the court case, I was chatting with my friend Krysta, who lives in Al Ain, an hour's drive from Dubai, and I asked her if I could come out to see her before the sentencing, and she was more than happy to have me. Two weeks later, Karla took me to the airport, and she told me to have a good time and relax. When I walked into the airport a wave of emotion hit me; tears filled my eyes, and I was trying not to cry. I was thinking it was unfair, Mero should have been with me. We both talked about going to see Krysta together. Mero got on so well with Krysta's children Ruby and Gabriel. Once through customs, I wiped my eyes and before I knew it I was on the plane. I was happy because I had three seats to myself, so I made a bed, watched a movie, and drank a Hennessey brandy for Mero. After the film, I took a sleeping pill, and when I woke up I was in Dubai.

Krysta was at work, so her friend picked me up and took me to her house. We'd worked together at Wilbraham Primary School where our friendship formed and we became good friends. When she got in from work, we hugged and laughed. It was so good to see her. Her kids came home from school and we chilled for the first night. The next morning, Krysta asked me what I was going to do that day while she was at work. I replied I was going to sunbathe on the rooftop, to which she told me it was very hot, and I asked if it was 'Kelly hot'. She said: 'You'll see.' I put my bikini on and went upstairs to the rooftop to soak up the sun, and to gather my thoughts about the sentencing after the trial. I must have been out there for five minutes before I had to go back inside. I've never felt heat like it before (dry desert heat). I filled a tub with cold water and went back to the rooftop, and every time I got hot I poured cold water over my body. While I was lying there, I heard a sound. It was quiet and soothing. I later found out it was called The Prayer. I stood up and looked around me. In the distance I could see the desert as Krysta's apartment was situated in Al Ain.

Krysta worked in a school and finished at one o'clock, which gave us plenty of time to do stuff in the day. We both freshened up and went to a bar called The Loft. It had a rooftop pool. We had food and drinks and had a good chat about Mero, sharing the memories we had of him. We laughed and cried, and every time we got hot, we cooled off in the pool. The weather in Dubai is so hot and the air so dry. That evening, Krysta invited Nimisha, her friend from work, to come over to the bar. Krysta introduced us and I told her all about Mero, and the day I received the phone call telling me he had been stabbed. We cried and then Krysta being Krysta made us laugh.

It was nice to be away from everything, and more importantly to be able to clear my thoughts and to be ready for the sentencing when I got back home. We stayed at The Loft until about eleven. The temperature had dropped, but it was still warm, and we were still in our swimming costumes and wrapped in towels. The next day, I was on the rooftop again trying to get a tan. It was peaceful and quiet up there; I loved it. That morning before she went to work, Krysta had asked me to leave the apartment door open so I could get back in. The dogs Mork and Mindy were already inside the apartment. During the morning, I listened to music, but I could hear the sound of a dog barking. I thought to myself that it sounded so clear, I knew the dogs were inside, but I got up and looked down from the rooftop and saw Mork the smaller dog, running around the carpark. I ran downstairs and tried to catch him, but he kept running away. I was worried, thinking Krysta was going to kill me if I didn't get the dog inside, and it took me at least ten minutes of chasing the dog until I finally managed to catch it and take it back inside. When Krysta came home, she joined me on the rooftop and I told her what had happened and we both laughed.

That evening, Krysta's friend Louise had invited us to dinner. We got dressed and took a taxi to her house. As soon as she opened the door, I immediately thought the house was amazing and it felt calming and peaceful. As we walked through to the garden, there were many statues of Buddha in different styles throughout the house. In the garden, Louise's partner was cooking. It was still very warm, and it was full of people. Even though I didn't know them, they were all very friendly. One woman I got talking to was telling me about her kids (this is one thing I found hard). She looked at me and asked if I had kids. I paused, and tears started falling down my cheeks. She said she was sorry and didn't mean to upset me. I told her it was okay, and then said that I had two boys, Remi and Mero, and that Mero had been murdered. She stared at me in shock and then she hugged me. All my emotions came flooding out, like a large wave, knocking me off my feet. Krysta came over, asking if I was okay. I said I was, I dried my tears and composed myself, but I found my thoughts drifting off, thinking about Mero, and the sentencing.

Krysta and I shared a bed during my stay with her, and at night we'd put the air conditioning on, and turn it off when we got cold, and every morning, there'd be a dog sleeping at the foot of the bed. We spent most of our time at The Loft, or the Rugby Club which also had a bar and a pool. Before I came home, I booked us in a hotel in Dubai for a night. We set off early and as we got close to Dubai, Krysta told me to look to my right, the buildings were tall, it was like entering into another world, it was beautiful and very clean. After checking in-the view from the room was amazing-we dropped our bags and went to the marina and had a cocktail while we watched the boats coming in and leaving. It was hot and I could barely take it all in, this place was amazing. We had a walk around the Dubai mall, where I saw the biggest fish tank in the world, and we shopped for gifts to bring back for the family.

Krysta knew what she was doing when she said we were going outside the mall. She told me to look up and there to my right was the Burj Khalifa; it was just beautiful. We found a restaurant and had dinner, while we were waiting for the Burj Khalifa to light up. I had a small picture card of Mero that I carried everywhere with me. I had a few of them because every time I visit somewhere in the world, I hide them, so it feels like Mero is visiting the place with me too. I told Krysta this and we walked closer to the building, trying to find a place where we could hide the picture. In the end we hid it underneath one of the posts.

We went back to the bar, and as we sat down, I saw Alison Hammond from *Good Morning Britain*, I went over to say hello and I had my picture taken with her. She was such a lovely lady. Once night had fallen, the Burj Khalifa was lit up and the fountains were switched on and the water moved in time to the music. It was such a beautiful thing to see. After the show we went back to the hotel and ordered food. We enjoyed the views and chilled. Of all the things we could have ordered, we settled on McDonalds, when it arrived, I was shocked by the amount of food; there were at least four burgers as well as nuggets and chips. When I had eaten, I fell asleep, and in the morning, I looked at the McDonalds bag and asked Krysta where the rest of the food had gone. She laughed and looked sheepish, during the night, she had woken up and ate all of the leftover food. She had been quiet because she didn't want to wake me. Krysta is that one friend who can make you laugh so much that your belly hurts and you end up crying as well.

We were going to spend the last day on the beach before going back to Al Ain. We stopped off at a local shop and brought some supplies for the day. We drove to the Jumeirah beach, where we set up our towels, and we sunbathed and were in and out of the sea. It was so hot, at one point we sat on the sand as the waves came over us, cooling us down. I asked Krysta if she would ever come back to Manchester. She looked at me and replied, 'Why would I, when I have all this?' Before we went back, Krysta took me to Jebel Hafeet, which was up a mountain, and when it was lit up at night, because it looked heavenly, people called it the pathway to heaven. I was quiet and scared as we drove up there because there were no crash barriers up the mountain. Once we reached the top, the views were out of this world, and we sat on a bench in the carpark, taking it all in. I was heading home the next day, and the ten days I'd spent in Dubai were just what I needed. I was looking forward to going home, to see Remi and my family, but not what was ahead of me - the sentencing of the defendants.

Chapter Twelve

27 May 2022 arrived, the day I had been dreading to face. I wanted the three individuals responsible for Mero's death to be given a long sentence, although no time would ever be enough because my baby has gone forever. I woke up at 7:30am, and I dressed in brown pants, a beige jumper, and a black and brown patterned jacket. I wanted to look my best because this was such an important day. I went downstairs and made a cup of tea and sat on the sofa. I went on Mero's Facebook page called Mero's World that I had created when he passed away, and I asked all of the followers to put up a purple heart in the hope that we would get the right and proper justice for Mero. I was so nervous and anxious, praying that the judge would give a hefty sentence, and I was also terrified because I was reading my Impact Statement in court, in front of everyone. As I waited for Claire, who worked for the police to arrive, my heart was beating so fast, when she arrived, she asked me if I was okay. I replied I was feeling scared and nervous, but I knew I had to do this for my baby. When we arrived at court, my other niece D'mornae, and my friends Karla, Paula and Fiona were there waiting for me.

We walked through the front doors and were searched by security, and then we made our way to the court. As we sat outside waiting to be called in, I noticed there was a heavy police presence when the families of the defendants arrived. The clerk appeared and told us we could go into court. We sat in the same place, and the defendants' families were sitting in the upper gallery. Before I left the house, I took a tablet for my anxiety. I needed to be calm before I read the Impact Statement out to the court.

The boys were led up from the cells, and once they were seated the judge read out his statement, and then I was asked by my son's barrister to stand up and to go into the witness box. The distance from where I was sitting to the witness box, felt like it was going to be one of the longest walks of my life. I felt that I couldn't do it, like my legs were going to give way on me. I managed to climb the three steps into the box, and I quickly looked around, at the families upstairs, the police and reporters to my right, the barristers in front of me, and then finally at Marquis, Giovanni, and Ryan in the box. All three were looking down, none of them able to look at me. The judge told me to look at him and read the statement to him. He gave me a focus, and I took a deep breath and read out my Impact Statement.

PERSONAL VICTIM STATEMENT

To the court my boy is just a statistic, just another case, but to me this is real life, it's my beautiful, fun loving, caring, respectable boy, who loved his family. On the ninth of September 2021 our lives were destroyed, receiving the phone call telling me that my son had been stabbed. It all seems so surreal, and it still does for all of us. At age sixteen, Rhamero is our youngest son, and had his whole life ahead of him. There were so many goals he wanted to achieve, goals that were taken away from him in such a cruel and horrific way.

Rhamero was looking forward to going to college, and even enjoyed his first day there. After college he was going to see his friends and he never made it home. We feel like this is all a bad nightmare and one we fear we won't wake up from.

Since Rhamero's death we have struggled both emotionally and physically. Each day is hard for us all, and we cannot come to terms with the loss of our baby. To get through each day, I now depend on medication for anxiety, and sleeping tablets to help me sleep, and my employer has referred me to their counselling service. My emotions are all over the place and I don't think I will ever come to terms with him not being here.

Rhamero's dad, Errol, is finding it hard mourning the loss of his youngest child. The last time he saw Rhamero was lying on a hospital bed, with his chest open, trying to be saved. This too was the last time his older brother Remi saw him. This is something Errol, Remi and I have to live with for the rest of our lives. His only nephew who is just two years old will now grow up just to know his uncle from photographs and stories we will tell him.

For all of those involved in taking my son's life, justice will prevail, and they will serve their time. However, during this time we know that they will still be able to have contact with their families, families who will never suffer in the way we have and will continue to suffer. And one day they will be released back into society, they will still be able to set and achieve goals, have a family, go on holiday and be around those that love them. This was taken away from Rhamero. Never again can we tell him we love him, that we're proud of him, or see him smash his life goals. Being so young when his life was taken in such an unethical way is hard to take, and something we will never be able to understand.

During the time we had to wait for Rhamero's body to be released for burial, he turned seventeen in heaven instead of here with his family. This broke us even more, as he was taken just over a week before his birthday. Our boy was laid to rest on 22 October 2021, a day before his brother's birthday. Remi is broken and cannot foresee a time when he can enjoy his birthday knowing he buried his little brother the day before, and we remain in this constant cycle of deep hurt and upset.

People tell us things like 'time will heal'. But how do we heal from this? Our son was murdered by these boys. People also say nice words, to try to help us accept Rhamero's death, and I say they will only ever understand when they have gone through the same process themselves. None of it seems real. Sometimes we get angry because they cannot even begin to understand what we're going through, and how it feels. The grief is unbearable. There has not been a single day we have managed to go through without breaking down and crying. Even the normal everyday things like going shopping and seeing items that Rhamero would like can just break you. We have had to move out of the area, away from the only house our family has ever called home, because there are too many memories. Having to pack Rhamero's belongings up in boxes knowing that he would not be moving with us was heart-breaking.

This was the first Christmas without Rhamero and we weren't looking forward to it. I didn't even want to put up the tree and decorations, without him helping me as he usually did, because he loved Christmas. This year I put up decorations with his face and name printed on them.

Losing a child is a different kind of grief; a piece of your heart is missing. We are doing a life sentence and things will never be the same for our family. Rhamero touched the lives of not just his family and friends, but the community too. I am constantly checking up on Remi, my older son, for the fear of losing another son is unbearable.

My nephew is going through counselling after Rhamero's death, because he thought it was going to happen to him and was afraid to leave his parents. Another nephew even asked his mum if Auntie Kelly was going to die like Mero.

Rhamero's death has had a massive impact on the family in so many ways. It has taken me three months to sleep in my own bed. Before this, I was sleeping on top of my bed, wrapping myself in Rhamero's duvet, just so I could smell him and be close to him. My appetite had deserted me; I can't eat, and I feel sick in my stomach knowing my boy isn't coming back.

This has hit us financially, as we are unable to work. Due to the shock and grief, we experience, we never know how we will be from one day to the next. Going from full-time work, I now stay at home trying to accept my son's death, and I don't even know when I will be able to return to some sort of 'normality'. We constantly ask why did four individuals want to kill our boy? Why did they chase him down and take his life?

My anxiety has hit a peak on the run up to this trial, knowing that we were going to have to relive Rhamero's last moments. How do we find any peace from this as his parents and family?

I strongly believe that it should be a life for a life. Justice shouldn't just be in the form of a few years behind bars. These boys hunted my son down like a pack of wolves, none of them considering the real impact not only on our family, but their families too. Hearing and watching the footage recorded during this trial has truly had a serious impact on me. My boy, who sounded so scared, and who tried to get away, not once but twice, will forever play in my head every time I close my eyes.

While at this time, I need those who are affected just as much as me - Errol, Rhamero's dad, and Remi, his brother - to be here with me to hear and see what has transpired in this court room, but I understand their broken hearts will not allow them to be here. I felt Mero was with me, giving me the strength to get through it. When I reached the end, I especially wanted to say something directly to Marquis, who had previously given a cut-throat gesture to me and my family. The whole court was silent when I spoke to Marquis. I stared straight at him and when I said his name, he looked up. 'You did a cut-throat gesture to me and my family and said 'Mero got smoked.' I then went on to say, 'Thank you for showing me what kind of person you are.' I looked at the judge and told him that I had finished and he said I could go back to my seat.

The judge then read out some more information and then spoke to the three defendants. 'Ryan Cashin, I sentence you to the minimum of twenty three years. Giovanni Lawrence, I sentence you to the minimum of twenty-one years. Marquis Richards, I sentence you to the minimum of eighteen years.' The defendant's families began to shout from the gallery above. We all gave loud sighs, and I said: 'Yes! Yes!' Liz, and Paul both smiled at me, and I smiled back. The judge told everyone to be quiet in court. A reporter from the Manchester Evening News stood up and asked the judge for permission to release the name of Marquis Richards to the press as well as on the news, as up to this time he couldn't be named because he was sixteen. When the judge gave his permission I was so happy, as I wanted all three of them to be named publicly. When the judge asked the guards to take the defendants to the cells, we all had to stand as the judge prepared to leave the court. I was praying that he would look at me, like all the other times just before he had gone into his chambers. As he was walking through the door, he stopped and turned around and looked straight at me. I raised my hands in prayer to him, and said thank you silently. He nodded and left the court.

Liz asked if I wanted to talk to the press who were waiting outside. I agreed, and while I was sitting in the waiting area, I phoned my sister, Errol, and Remi to tell them the sentences the boys received. We waited for the families of the boys to leave and then I walked out of court alone, to the reporters who were waiting on the steps, Claire, Liz and Paul came to stand behind me. 'Just don't carry a knife,' I said. 'It's like a ripple effect. You're not only affecting victims, but you're also affecting families, their friends, even down to the community. Rhamero's death has affected so many lives. It needs to stop, enough is enough, put down the knives! From start to finish, these individuals have shown no remorse, or respect. This is real life; they took my son's life!'

After speaking to the press, we all got into our cars and left. One of the first places I went to was to Cheetham Hill to buy fireworks and purple flares. My friends Karla and Nicola drove to the balloon shop to buy purple balloons with Mero's name printed on them. I put a post on Facebook letting everyone know that we received justice for Mero, and I was overwhelmed to see how much love from everyone posting purple hearts on his page. I asked family and friends to meet me in Fallowfield at 6:00pm, to let off the balloons and the flares for Mero. We met near the school Mero attended and at the spot near our old family home, where there is a triangle at the junction between Hart Road and Whitmore Road. When we let the fireworks off, Remi and I also let off the purple balloons. My cousin Claire started crying, and then she shouted: 'Whose world is it?' We all replied: 'Mero's world!'

I drove home with Paula, not knowing how to feel. Yes, we finally had closure for my baby boy. I don't like saying justice has been served because me and my family are serving the life sentence not having Mero with us any longer. I thought it was all over; well, certainly the fight was and the boys who murdered my son were behind bars for years to come. Just close family and friends came back to my house for a drink. I had a Hennessey for my baby boy, feeling now I could breathe a bit easier, and that my son can rest and be at peace.

Chapter Thirteen

September seemed to come around too soon. It was a month I used to love, with it being Mero's birthday month, but now I dread it when it comes. Mero's anniversary was coming up, the first year without my baby boy. I kept on thinking to myself, *has a year really gone that fast without my boy?* It still feels like it was yesterday, and I wasn't sure what I wanted to do for it. Work was beginning on the mural on Norton Street, and I wanted to be there, and so I went with Toni and Deanne. Amy Coney, the artist, was already at the site. We introduced ourselves and she gave me a hug. She had already painted in the shape of the sun on the wall, and I asked if I could get on the crane and help with the spraying. Amy agreed. I put on a harness, for health and safety reasons, and went up on the crane. I felt happy being a part of things, spraying yellow and orange paint on the wall. Amy was doing her best to finish it for Mero's anniversary on the ninth, but the wet weather was holding her back.

9 September 2022 arrived. The sun was shining, and I woke up feeling that I wanted to stay busy. The family arranged for us to meet at the cemetery for drinks and food and to let off balloons for Mero. Before I met up with the family, I went to Norton Street to lay some flowers, along with the flowers the residents from the street had previously placed, which was nice to see. I met Caron and Kate there and played 'Baby Boy' from my car and had a cry with them. From there I went on to the cemetery,

where I met up with family and Mero's friends. The turnout was beautiful. We all had a Hennessey shot for Mero, let off purple flares and balloons with his name on, and had food and played music at his grave. We stayed there for a couple of hours and then everyone came back to my house, where we all relaxed in the back garden, having a drink for Mero, and when it got dark we let off three lanterns for him and the fireworks.

Mero's mural was nearly finished, and I asked my friend Quinton Green if he could write a poem for the mural, with a QR code next to it so people would be able to listen to the poem about Mero. He was honoured to write the poem, and I sent photos and special memories of Mero, as well as Amy's drawing plans for the mural. A few days later it was the launch date for the mural and Quinton's poem. I went to Norton Street with family and friends.

Unfortunately, Amy, the artist, couldn't make it, but I met Linda from Old Trafford Creative. I was blown away with the final piece, I was amazed at how beautiful it looked. Linda asked me if I noticed anything on the mural, and I saw the purple heart. Amy said she wanted to make the area where I had sprayed stand out by painting in a purple heart in the tree, and I thought it was thoughtful of Amy to do this for me. The mural was perfect for my boy, and going to Norton Street made it that bit easier seeing the mural, which was thanks to Maggie for making it happen.

The crowd had gathered, and I had written a speech especially for the occasion, but when I opened my mouth, I felt there was something stuck in my throat. I paused and started to cry, and I said to my niece, Deanne that she would have to read the speech for me. A man in the crowd said: 'Come on, Kelly, you can do it.' My cousin Claire said that we had all the time in the world and that they would wait for me. It just broke my heart being on Norton Street, the place where Mero was hurt. I managed to compose myself and read out my speech. I thanked everyone for coming and then played Quinton's poem through a speaker, so we all could hear it as we looked at Mero's mural. Everyone had tears in their eyes after listening to the poem. It touched a part of my heart in a different way. It was more powerful to watch the video Quinton had put together, and I couldn't thank him enough. Quinton and I became good friends after meeting on Facebook. He was also campaigning to raise awareness on knife crime. He would always send me messages, or phone to check in on how I was doing. I've met some amazing people on Facebook who have helped and supported me, and still do. Zoe reached out to me straight away after she had learned what had happened to Mero, Zoe lost her son Byron, Julie lost her grandson, Liam, Jeanine lost her son Tyrelle, Janine lost her son Teon, Nanny Viv lost her grandson Marni, and Joanie lost her son Kennie months after I lost Mero. These mums understood my pain and loss in so many ways. They became my safety net, and when I needed someone to talk to, they were there.

After just getting over the first anniversary of Mero not being here with me, I had to face another birthday without him, his 18th birthday. Remi had always said he wanted to take Mero away to Amsterdam for his

18th birthday, so Remi and I decided to go together, for Mero. The day before Mero's birthday, I went to the cemetery knowing I wasn't going to be there on the actual day. I brought big balloons with 18 printed on them, put up birthday banners on his grave, and brought him a beautiful bunch of purple flowers. I stayed there for about an hour, playing music to him.

When I got home, I got ready for Amsterdam, where we were going for the day. We got an early night, as we had to be at the airport for 7:00am. The next morning when my alarm woke me up, I sat up in bed and said: 'Happy Birthday, son, love you forever.' I knew Mero would have wanted us to enjoy this day for him. We got an Uber to the airport, and we slept on the plane, and when we woke up, we were in Amsterdam. Before getting on a train to the town centre, we took a picture standing next to the Amsterdam sign outside the airport. It was my first time visiting there, but Remi had been a couple of times before. We didn't have long to wait for the train, which ran every 15 minutes, and the journey into the centre took us 20 minutes.

The weather was warm, and we decided to go and find a café to have breakfast. We found a nice one facing the canal. I tucked into a full English, and Remi had nuggets and chips. Once we'd eaten, Remi led and I followed. Amsterdam is a lovely place to visit. We went to Madame Tussauds, shopped, and visited a café, where Remi smoked and I had a drink for my baby boy's birthday. I brought some picture cards of Mero and we stuck them up wherever we went. We had a lot of walking ahead of us, as Remi didn't want to hire a bike. We sat down in the city square and watched a man performing magic tricks. He was really funny and had the crowd laughing. It was nice spending some quality time with Remi, but it ended all too soon, as we had food and then took the train back to the airport. Remi had a little nap as we waited for our flight back, and I was on my phone, keeping myself busy. When we were about to board after an hour of waiting, my phone charger wasn't working and my phone was about to die, and we panicked, because our boarding passes were on the phone. In the end I asked a young girl if I could borrow her charger, and I was able to charge my phone enough to show our boarding passes, and we boarded the plane and headed back home to Manchester.

Chapter Fourteen

Life just got busier with running the charity, and the Youth Hub once a week, installing cabinets, and holding events to raise money. I was receiving invites to meetings with the Violence Reduction Unit, knife crime events, and going into schools and colleges to raise awareness about knife crime. One particular school I went to was Baguley Primary School with Jeanine, who had also lost her son to knife crime. We shared our stories and then at the end I spoke about the bleed safety cabinet. The school wanted to help raise money for one to be installed at the local shop near their school, and one pupil, Lottie, wrote to all the parents whose child attended the school and asked for their help to raise the money. In time they were able to achieve it and with my help, a cabinet was installed. It is important to raise awareness when children are at primary school age to talk about the importance of not carrying knives, not to mention the ripple effects it has on the families before they make the transition into high school.

On another occasion I ran a workshop at Bury College with Roy, Karl, Graham, and Jeanine. I walked into the room and my heart sank as I looked at the rows of chairs. I asked the headmaster how many pupils were attending the workshop, and he said 380. I have never spoken in front of that many people before, and as the pupils started coming in, my palms were sweating and my nerves started to get the better of me. Jeanine assured me that I would be fine, and Roy started the workshop without telling me he had added a video of Mero. Watching Mero on the video gives people an idea of who he was as a person, and my eyes filled with tears watching it. When it was my turn to stand up and speak, I told them of the day I received the awful phone call. I held on to the mic tightly, as my palms were sweating, and I stared at the audience, who were silent as I told my story. I couldn't wait to sit back down, and once we were finished, the headmaster asked if there were any questions for me and the other speakers. When I turned round, there was a long line of pupils wanting to hug me, and to tell me how strong I was. One boy just stared at me and then saluted me, saying how strong I was and how sorry he was for the loss of my boy. The feedback I received was overwhelming. If I can get through to one child, then I am doing something right.

We were continuing to receive recognition from those who'd heard about Mero's World and what we were doing around Greater Manchester. We were even invited to have afternoon tea with the Lord Mayor, who thanked us for setting up our charity. Don't get me wrong, the recognition is nice, but for me it's about saving lives and preventing another parent from going through the same loss and pain that I am still going through.

It was coming up to a year since we buried Mero, and the day before was Remi's 25th birthday. It felt bittersweet because I had lost a son but I still wanted to make Remi's day special. My emotions were up and down, and I knew I had to focus all my energies on Remi; however, Remi being Remi, he hates any fuss and being the centre of attention. So I had to tell

117

him I was organising a party for him, or he wouldn't have turned up; that's my child all over! Anyway, he agreed and we held it at a bar in town. After getting ready, I came downstairs, and I found our dog Draco had just licked the side of Remi's birthday cake! I called Remi to come downstairs to see what Draco had done and we both laughed and said, 'It is what it is.' I asked Remi's girlfriend Sadie if she could pick me up a cake. Off we went to the venue, which was filled with everyone who loved and cared for him. What a night we had. We partied until the early hours. Seeing my son happy and letting his hair down after losing his little brother was so good to see. People were on the dance floor, dancing and having fun. Remi grabbed the mic and started mc-ing and joking around, but I knew deep down he wanted his little brother there. Nearly one week later, I received an email from the Be Proud Awards, saying that someone had nominated our charity for an award. The ceremony was going to take place in March 2023, which was still a way off. I was able to invite another person, and I was straight on the phone asking my niece, Deanne, if she would come with me.

Things were moving so quickly. I received a call from Jacqui from Reel MCR, saying their launch for the documentary was coming up and they wanted me to be involved. I agreed and went along with my cousin Claire and a friend Nicola. The Violence Reduction Unit were there with all the other people who took part. It was held at The Lowry Hotel. We had a cup of tea and pastries while we were waiting to be called into the main room. When Jacqui appeared, she told me to sit at the front, and I asked Nicola and Claire to sit behind me. They played the film, which was called *No Safe Place*, and when it had ended, the two producers stood up and gave a speech; then it was my turn. I was feeling nervous because the room was filled with important people. I stood up and introduced myself, and told them I had lost my son to knife crime in September 2021, and I thanked them for coming and sat down quickly. I was presented with a bouquet of flowers to say thank you for my involvement. The video is now available to watch on YouTube.

Christmas was approaching, the second one without Mero, but the first one in our new home. Christmas will never be the same again for me. I try to make it fun for my grandson Caerus. I used to love the build up to it, and was so organised with everything, from buying presents to sorting out the food for Christmas dinner. Things changed dramatically after Mero's death. Christmas Eve was spent with Remi, Sadie, and Caerus. We watched Caerus open his Christmas Eve box from Mero (I did this as a little gift from Mero). After a while Remi said he wasn't feeling too well and went to bed, leaving me with Sadie and Caerus. We stayed up, had a drink, and let off some fireworks for Mero, while saying a Happy Christmas to him. Since his death, on any occasion I always let fireworks off for him. We went to bed and the next morning, Christmas Day, in my eyes, it was just a normal day. We went downstairs and watched Caerus open his presents, I made breakfast, and mid-afternoon Sadie left with Caerus to see her family.

Remi went back to bed, and I got dressed because I was going to my sister's house for dinner. Before going I stopped at the cemetery and spent some time with Mero. I put some flowers down, and I didn't stay too long because it was cold. As I drove to my sister's house, I thought it was rubbish not spending the day with my boys. At my sister's house, things were relaxed; we watched Christmas films and ate our Christmas dinner. I left early in the evening to bring Remi some food, but he wasn't in the mood to eat. I spent the rest of the evening in bed, watching television and flicking through my phone.

Chapter Fifteen

As a charity we wanted to do something that covered all levels of those who had lost their lives through knife crime in Manchester. We decided to do an Angel Walk in Fallowfield. We proposed to start the walk at Holy Trinity Church on Platt Lane, walk down the length of Platt Lane to The Place at Fallowfield Library, to the bleed safety cabinet - the first one we had installed for Mero, which also has a plaque on it. On the morning of the walk, we asked everyone to meet at Holy Trinity Church. Mothers and families who have experienced loss to knife crime came to show their support, and to unite as one. Councillor Jade Doswell, Afzal Khan MP, the Lord Mayor of Manchester, Donna Ludford, and Deputy Mayor, Kate Green all came to give their support. It was the first time I met Quinton Green, but when he got out of his car, it felt like I had known him all my life.

When the crowd assembled, it was time to start the walk. Families held pictures of their loved ones, and I had a picture of my prince as we walked. Cars and people were stopping to look at us. Many people knew who I was and what I was doing because of Mero. We stopped outside the bleed cabinet and then Jade, Kate, Afzal, and Donna all gave short speeches, before we all headed back to the church for a service. Paul Mathole took the service. The church was important to me because it's the church that blessed Mero when he was born and the one where he was laid to rest. Pictures of those who have lost their lives to knife crime were placed on the stage, as well as candles. The priest started the service, and then Keena and Neffie read out all the victims' names, followed by Quinton's poems, and I finished it off with a speech, thanking everyone for coming.

After the service, which was both powerful and beautiful, we had refreshments so the families could come together. I was still in disbelief that I was doing this, sitting with other mothers and supporting them, because we had lost our sons. Later that night we were taking Quinton out, because he was staying in Manchester for the night. I got dressed and Deanne, Gaynor and Quinton and I headed for the city centre, where Neffie and Jane would meet us to celebrate Jane's birthday. In the taxi, Quinton was entertaining us with his MC skills. We went for some food and then we met up at a roller disco, where we had fun roller skating and drinking cocktails. We went on to another bar, and then at about midnight, I took an Uber home.

I was spending the next morning with Quinton before he headed home. We had food, and as we were near the cemetery I asked if he wanted to go to see Mero's grave. He replied that it would be an honour, and we both sat on Mero's bench, looking at his grave. Later, I asked if he wanted to go to Mero's mural. We did and he read a poem for Mero in front of the mural. We took pictures, and then it was time for Quinton to go home. I made a friend for life in Quinton; he lifts me up when I am feeling low, and he's just always there for me.

The awards night was here before I knew it, and I found out it was Keena, Errol's cousin who had nominated us for an award. I had my make-up done earlier in the day and then chilled in the afternoon until it was time to go. I wore a black velvet dress, with silver heels. Deanne came to my house, and we took a taxi to the Midland Hotel in Manchester city centre, where the award ceremony was being held. We met Keena and Gaynor at the hotel, and we took pictures before we went into the hotel. There was a red carpet, which made us feel very important. We weren't allowed to go into the room and had to wait in the reception area, where we were served Prosecco. I went to look at the seating plan to see where we would be sitting. Keena and Gaynor chatted to the other community groups. The drinks were going down well and we were feeling nervous, and excited.

A man came out of the room and announced that we could now go and sit at our tables. The décor was nice; white tablecloths and black chairs. The stage was at the front with two large screens on either side so the audience could see the nominees. There were bottles of wine on the table, as well as booklets that showed that there were nine award categories. We ate a beautiful two-course meal: I had the chicken and potatoes and vegetables, with chocolate cake to finish. One waitress approached me saying that she had gone to school with Mero and that she was sorry to hear of his death, and she told us that her mum follows us on Facebook. I was sitting next to a gentleman called Gareth Worthing, who wasn't up for an award himself, but was there to accept an award on behalf of his friend if he won, who couldn't make it. Gareth and I chatted and I told him about the bleed cabinets we as a charity had been installing in Manchester. He gave me his number and said he would see what he could do to help us. He was a funny guy and kept us entertained throughout the evening.

Our category was the sixth category, and the speaker informed us that the award was for the charity that was working to create safer neighbourhoods, and he then read out the nominees. The other speaker said they had chosen the winner for their amazing drive and to make a difference in the face of great personal tragedy through fund raising, creating a charity, and doing so much more to raise awareness. At this point I must have been in a daze with it all, and then Keena kept saying, 'We've done it.' Then I heard, 'It gives me great pleasure to announce the winner of Creating Safer Neighbourhoods is Kelly Brown, for the Mero's World Foundation.' I put my head down, not believing it was our first award for my boy's charity. Deanne, Gaynor, Keena and I walked to the stage, Donna Ludford, the Lord Mayor of Manchester, stopped me and we hugged, and she congratulated me. Once on the stage, we were presented with a framed certificate, and also a framed picture that showed a young person standing next to a sign which showed how many casualties had happened so far in Manchester. It was a powerful message.

When all the awards had been given out, there was another award which was the Be Proud Award. The speaker was talking on the stage, but I wasn't paying too much attention, because I was still in shock for winning an award. I messaged Remi, Sadie, and Naomi to let them know I had won an award, and they were so happy that I had won. Then out of nowhere, all I heard was 'Kelly Brown'. I thought.

There's only one Kelly Brown in here, and when I looked up, everyone was cheering. In that split second, I felt like I wasn't there. I had tears in my eyes as Gaynor hugged me, and as I headed for the stage, the cheering grew louder. As I stood on the stage, I was in disbelief, feeling overwhelmed that I had won two awards in one night.

I was presented the award by Javeno Mclean, who had won the award last year. He had followed his heart and opened a gym exclusively for people with dementia and other disabilities. When I got on stage, he hugged me and told me how proud he was of my work, I was presented with a framed certificate with the words 'Be Proud of Manchester', and because I was the overall winner on the night, I received a huge picture of a man holding up a golden trophy. I was shown over to the end of the stage where I had a photo taken with Javeno, and then on my own. At this point I was amazed and blown away, and when I got back to my seat I phoned my family again to tell them I had won a second award.

We enjoyed a few more drinks, me being on the brandy, of course. Although people were beginning to leave the room, we stayed at our table and chatted. The cleaners came in and asked if we were ready to leave because they wanted to start clearing away. I looked at them and jokingly said: 'Do you know who we are? We're Be Proud of Manchester winners.' We left our awards with the receptionist and headed for the bar where we had more drinks. Gareth was with his partner. We had met them both earlier in the evening, and he brought us a drink before leaving, and we stayed at the bar, having a laugh. Keena was keeping us all amused, and at one point she went to the toilet, and when she was on her way back, she walked past our table, forgetting where we were.

At midnight, we decided to call it a night and ordered our taxis. Our driver took one look at me and said the picture was bigger than me. We laughed and then asked him if he knew who we were. We replied, 'Proud of Manchester!' On the ride home, I was happy that I had a perfect ending to a wonderful night, and I gave one of the pictures to Deanne, and I couldn't wait to show Remi what we had won. I put the certificates and the large picture in Mero's room, where they belong. I won them for him, because it's him that's giving me the strength to make the change. The next morning, I woke up to my face all over The Manchester Evening News for Mero's World winning two awards in one night.

Chapter Sixteen

Our Youth Hub was going from strength to strength, and funding from Youth and Play allowed us to buy resources for the children, like boxing gloves, a PlayStation 5, and board games etc. We always provide light snacks for the children while they are at the Hub, and we also have a tuck shop selling sweets, crisps, and drinks at cheaper prices than the local shops because of the rising costs of living. We paid for people to come in and hold boxing training for the children.

We also received funding from the Violence Reduction Unit for a youth mentor called Matthew. He worked with the kids to build a relationship with him, allowing them to open up and talk to him. Matthew and I have similar backgrounds he too has lost someone close to him, his brother Gary, through knife crime. Matthew and I became good friends. He understands my passion to make a change and to help the next generation. He has a good heart and a caring soul, which is why he is so successful at what he does, in helping kids on a daily basis. He is someone who inspires me in every way possible, by always giving me advice when I'm going into schools to do my workshops, suggesting ways I can help Mero's World to grow as a foundation. One of his ideas was to do 'lives' on Facebook with other mothers. I followed it through and once a week I speak to a different mother, giving them the opportunity to share their story of losing their son. It's also about raising awareness because the public at large don't know or even understand the impact it has on the families. Until you hear it first-hand from the grieving mothers, who are still going through all this pain. It never goes away, and it doesn't get easier; we just learn to deal with it, in our own ways.

After Mero had passed, we had spoken to the Violence Reduction Unit, who gave Odd Arts funding to create a short film about Mero and knife crime. My head was filled with other things at the time, and I almost forgot about it. I got in touch with Becky at Odd Arts and asked if the funding was still available. She informed us that it still was, so Deanne and I arranged to meet her to talk. We had changed our minds about what we had previously agreed we wanted, because we were doing so much work with the bleed cabinets, and because I was a visual learner, we came up with the idea of a short film on how to use the bleed safety cabinets.

Lance and Jai came to the Hub one evening to do some filming for the video, and brought along the Street Doctors, who taught the children general first aid. While Ros, Jai and Lance worked on the video, Becky and I worked on a launch day for the release of the video. We decided to hold the launch at the Whitworth Art Gallery. We invited the Violence Reduction Unit, because they had given the funding to make the video, and we also invited the Street Doctors, and members of the community. We set up a large screen in one of the event rooms, put out tables and chairs and also laid on refreshments. Prior to the event, I was sent a preview copy of the video. I was impressed with the end result, and I also got to meet some of the actors who were involved in the filming. Becky gave a talk about putting the video together, and after the film was aired, I thanked everyone for coming, and then Deanne talked the audience through the cabinet, the contents inside it, and more importantly how to use it. We also asked the audience to scan the QR code and to share the video on YouTube. I shared the video on all the social media platforms of Mero's World to advertise the cabinets and how easy they were to use, and how important they are to save lives.

With all of this going on, it was keeping my mind occupied; it was giving me a focus and a purpose. I booked a holiday with my friends to Portugal. I felt like I needed to switch off and focus on me. I was meeting Paula and Gaynor at the airport on the morning of the holiday. I ordered my Uber, said goodbye to Remi and set off for the airport. I arrived at Terminal 3 and phoned Gaynor, asking where she was. She said she was there waiting for me, I phoned Paula and asked where she was. She replied that she and Gaynor were together, waiting for me. I began to feel stressed and went to the front desk and asked which terminal I was in. It turned out I was in the wrong terminal - I should have been in Terminal 1. At this point I was stressing, and I wanted to go home. Paula said she would come over to meet me. A man who was standing nearby had overheard my conversation and told me he was in the wrong terminal too! He offered to take me to the correct terminal and on the way, I bumped into Paula. We finally got to the check in desk, and we discovered our luggage was overweight, so we had to pay the surcharge. I couldn't wait to get to the lounge to have a drink, but we couldn't because there was no time left. Finally, we boarded the plane, and I was able to have my Hennessey!

I was with a group of girls, and we were staying in two town houses. I shared mine with Kirstie and her husband, Steven. The holiday was just what I needed. It was a party week; we had a laugh, going to pool parties, beach parties, and each day we were meeting new people. Everyone was getting sick of me in the town house, because I constantly wanted my picture taken in different locations and outfits. Steve didn't mind; he was like my personal photographer, as well as a joker, and he treated me like his daughter. He and Kirstie constantly checked in on me, making sure I was eating and that I was okay, Steven also helped me hide Mero's picture cards in different places. Kirstie and I have been friends for years. We first met in a hair salon, where she was one of the hairdressers and I was a junior, and our friendship grew from there. We hadn't seen each other for a long time, but she was always there in the background if I needed her.

The weather in Portugal was hot, hotter than normal, and I spent the day in my bikini soaking up the sun and relaxing. Steven and Kirstie, who I called my holiday mum and dad, cooked for us. When Kirstie did the cooking, she left a mess behind. I couldn't cope with the mess and in the end, I did the cleaning up after her. One day, I locked my keys inside my suitcase with my bag and money. Trying to get it open was a nightmare. There was a small hole at the top and I was trying to squeeze my hand inside it. Bev, who was staying in the other town house, tried to get inside my case but couldn't. Trying to get inside my suitcase was comical. I was fuming, because I'd damaged my handbag in the process, and in the end, Steven came to the rescue. He managed to open my case with a pair of scissors.

After sunbathing on the first day of our holiday, we went to the supermarket to buy supplies. We were told it was a ten-minute walk away, but it ended up being more like twenty minutes. We decided to order an Uber for the journey back after shopping. On the taxi ride back to our house, I was in one of my daft moods. I was pretending to the taxi driver that Steven and Kirstie were my parents. I asked Steven if I could have a drink that night, and he replied, going along with the joke, that I could drink the whole bottle. The face of the taxi driver was a picture, and we all laughed and laughed, which was good for me to be able to relax and be okay with laughing.

Justina, a member of our party, had also suffered the death of her son. He was killed a few months before we flew out. I wanted to make the night at the beach special for her, so after the beach party, I gathered our party together. We wrote their names in the sand surrounded by love hearts, and wrote messages on the two lanterns, one for Zikel and one for Mero and we set them off. Zikel's rose into the air and drifted away, whereas Mero's wouldn't rise; it just glided across the sand. I had to smile, and I said, 'Mero was being stubborn, not wanting to go anywhere.' Justina and I hugged each other and cried for our boys. We were feeling each other's pain. People who were passing by stopped and asked what we were doing. We explained that the ceremony was for our boys, and they had tears in their eyes and hugged us. It was quite an emotional evening, but perfect for our boys.

Seven days were up, and some of our party were leaving. Paula and Gaynor and I were staying on for another three days. I was glad that I had more time to soak up the sun. It was while I was sunbathing I received a phone call from an unknown number. It was from a woman who introduced herself as Pav. I kindly asked her to ring back in a few days' time, as I was on holiday and needed the break. She was from Manchester BBC Radio, and I assumed she was ringing in relation to knife crime. We enjoyed the next few days with sightseeing, buying gifts and eating out, and when the ten days were up. I was ready to go back to see Remi and my family, I was also organising an event for our charity reaching its one year anniversary and I wanted to make the event special.

When I was finally at home, I received another call from Pav and found out that I had been nominated for another award. This time it was a bravery award given by BBC Manchester Radio. I was grateful that someone had nominated me, and this time I chose the dress I was going to wear with care, as this meant more to me. This was about everything that I'd gone through with the loss of Mero and fighting for change, so I went online and searched for a dress. I had a month before the awards. I put all my focus into the charity event we were holding. We sold tickets and were going to hold a raffle, and all the monies raised were going to purchase more cabinets around Manchester. I phoned St Kentigern's, the local

Irish social club in Fallowfield. I spoke to Ryan and explained why we wanted to hire the club. He expressed his sympathy and told us we could have the club free of charge, as he knew Mero from the local area. We booked the club for 25 August 2023. Tickets started selling well and we began preparing for the night: asking for the community to donate the raffle prizes, organising the food and the deejay, as well as finding the prefect dress, and once everything was organised, I was finally able to relax.

I had another holiday booked; this time it was four days away to Fuengirola in Spain. I went with my friends Karla, Jo and Hayley. Originally, I was supposed to be going to Canada to stay with my Auntie Sandra, who was married to my dad's brother, Ray. She had sent me the money for my flight, but because my visa didn't come through in time, I couldn't go, so she sent me the money to go on holiday with my friends instead. We were flying out in the morning, so I stayed at Karla's house to make things easier, as Jo lived next door, and Hayley would come in a taxi. When we arrived at the airport, we checked our luggage in and then went to the VIP lounge for breakfast, with of course, a glass of brandy and Coke; it would have been rude not to start the holiday off that way. We stayed in the lounge until it was time to board the plane. As we were walking to the boarding gate, we heard the final call for our flight, and we all started running to the gate.

As I was walking on the tarmac towards the plane, I said to the girls, 'Isn't it mad that we trust one guy with our lives?' They looked at me and told me to shut up, and we started laughing. When we had boarded the plane, I saw a guy dressed like a pilot, and I asked him if he was the pilot. He replied that he was, and then out of nowhere, and maybe because I was feeling in a giddy mood, I said, 'Aww, isn't he cute?' Jo was embarrassed; she couldn't believe what I had just said, and Karla just told me to sit down, and the people sitting in the seats near to us all laughed at what I'd said. Once we'd arrived, I was sharing with Karla, while Jo and Hayley were next door.

With it still being early, we put our bikinis on and went down to the pool. The weather was very hot, and we were glad that we had gone for the all-inclusive holiday because all the drinks were free. We tried a few different cocktails, and Jo and I fell in love with the Blue Lagoon. After a few of them I went into the pool, while Jo sat at the edge with her feet dangling in the water. We were deep in conversation, talking about life and Mero. The time just flew by, and Karla came over and asked if we wanted to go for a walk. We were very tipsy from the cocktails and the heat, and as we walked, we joked and laughed. I could hear birds that sounded like the birds from Manchester. I looked up and saw a parakeet, and I joked to the girls it was the same one that flew around Fog Lane Park.

The next day we decided to spend the day on the beach. It was within walking distance from our hotel, and we hired two four-poster sunbeds. The sun was scorching, and every time I needed to cool down, I'd go to the shower and then go back to sunbathing. During the day, I'd wind up the girls by calling the Lucky-Lucky Men, who were selling stuff to come over. I said to one that Jo wanted to buy a handbag. I was laughing so much because Jo was pretending to be asleep, and then I did the same to Karla. After having food, we went back to the beach. I really wanted to try paragliding, but none of the girls wanted to try it, so we went into the sea instead. It was cold at first, but once our bodies got used to it, we swam further out. The atmosphere on the beach was fantastic and chilled. People were swimming and sunbathing and having fun. We left the beach at six and went back to our hotel to freshen up for our evening meal, and that evening we went to the strip and visited a couple of bars and had more cocktails. We decided to chill by the pool the next day, and after putting our towels on the sunbeds, we went for breakfast, and with it being all-inclusive, I couldn't complain because each day there was a variety of food on offer.

Hayley grew bored of me mentioning the parakeet and blue lagoons and jokingly said I wasn't allowed to mention them again. That evening we got dressed and took a taxi into the old town. It was lively and very busy compared to where we were staying. We had a walk around and Hayley got her hair braided. We decided it was too busy, so we had one drink and got a taxi back to the hotel to see what entertainment they were offering, which was nothing exciting, so we called it a night. On our last day, we had a beach day and hired the same sunbeds. A Chinese man approached us, asking us if we wanted a massage. Karla and I said we did, and the full body massage I received was firm and very relaxing. The only thing I didn't like was when he pulled my toes apart. We spent the day laughing, drinking cocktails and enjoying ourselves. Later, we went to the strip to buy presents, and then we had an early night ready to fly home in the morning.

Chapter Seventeen

Installing the bleed cabinets around Manchester couldn't have happened without the help from Michael. He was the caretaker at the school where I used to work. I first approached Michael and asked if he would install the first ever cabinet in memory of Rhamero in Fallowfield. He said it would be an honour to do that and to put up the plaque too. It took him hours to install it and he confided that he felt under pressure because he wanted to get it right for Mero. Since installing the first one in February 2022, we have been on many road trips from as far as Heywood, to Withington, Old Trafford and Rusholme. The more experience Michael had in installing the forty-nine cabinets and packs, the more confident and quicker he became. He was able to put them up in strong winds, and heavy rain.

Our road trips all over Manchester have been really amusing, with many stories. One of the funniest was when we were going to install a cabinet outside the shops near Gorse Hill Studios. I was driving down Chester Road and I had to pull over because I heard a noise. I discovered that I had a flat tyre, and I decided to drive on to a tyre place I knew five minutes away. I set off, driving slowly with my hazards flashing. My tyre was getting flatter, and I started to panic, especially with the long line of traffic forming behind me. I saw a petrol station and pulled into it and put more air into the tyre. While I went to the shop, Michael filled the tyre with air. When I returned, he asked what I had done to the tyre as there was more than just one puncture. I laughed, and thought of an idea, which was to stick the gum I had just bought and was chewing onto the tyre to block up the hole, and I used a wet wipe to block the other hole. He looked at me and laughed, asking what I was doing, and I replied that I was trying to stop the air escaping from the tyre. We laughed, and Michael said that it summed up my personality, trying to find the positives in life. We got back into the car and drove to the tyre shop, where they said it was going to take at least thirty minutes to fix the punctures.

We left the car and walked the short distance to Chester Road, where we met Andy and Katie; however, when we reached the location, we found there was no room to install the cabinet. I decided that I wasn't going home with the cabinet, and asked the landlord of the Gorse Hill, the pub nearby if we could put it up outside his pub. He said they didn't get trouble there and asked how much it was going to cost. When I assured him, it was free, he agreed. When the cabinet was installed, I went into the pub to give the landlord the code. He told me that there were a lot of kids in the area with knives, and one of his locals had told him that he'd sent his child to school once with a knife. I thought, *What the hell is this world coming to*? But I was glad there was a cabinet there now. The man who ran the takeaway next door invited us in and gave us free food, which was more than welcome. The tyre took another hour to be fixed, as it had to be ordered in from another place. I was glad to get home, thinking what a day it had turned out to be.

The following day while I was sitting at home, I was thinking about Mero's belongings, where they were being stored and wondering if I could get them back. I called Paul Davies and asked him how I should go about it. He told me he would make some inquiries and get back to me. He phoned me shortly after and said he would bring Mero's bag to me, but he was still waiting to find out about his clothes. A couple of days later, Paul came to my house. He asked how I was, and I replied that I was okay, and when we sat down, he handed me a gold and white box. He said he didn't want to give the bag like that to me, so he brought a box to put it in. He also said that due to the forensic examination, the chemicals they had used had discoloured the bag. I told him that was okay, and I opened the box, but I closed it straight away. I didn't know what I was feeling at that moment in time, but I knew I didn't want the police to have Mero's belongings. I asked Paul if I could have his clothes. He asked me if I was sure, because some of the clothes were cut when he was in the hospital. I said it was fine, and he said he would bring them to me. When he left, I didn't look into the box again. I put it in Mero's room with the rest of his clothes.

A couple of days later, Paul returned with Mero's clothes. As he pulled up outside the house, my heart started racing, and I was wondering if I really wanted to see them after nearly two years. I opened the door and Paul carried in large see-through police forensic bags, secured with ties, but I could still see Mero's clothes. He asked if I was okay, and I replied that I thought I was. He told me Mero's hoodie had been in the freezer, and was still frozen, in another bag were his black socks, boxers, grey Nike trainers, black North Face pants, and white plain t-shirt. I'd honestly forgotten what he was wearing on that last day, and seeing the clothes brought it all painfully back to me. I noticed there was blood on Mero's trainers, and my heart skipped a beat, and because I had fallen quiet, Paul asked me if I was okay again. I replied that I was trying to take it all in.

When he left, I sat back down, and stared at the bags, trying to avoid looking at the clothes inside. Finally, I took them upstairs and put them in my bedroom. Remi walked in and asked what was in the bags. I said they were Mero's clothes. He picked up the bag that held Mero's trainers in and when he saw the blood, he put it down straight away, saying that he couldn't look at it. I explained that was why I was keeping them in my room, as I wanted to protect him, but he didn't agree; he said I should keep them in Mero's room and reminded me that he was grown.

The next morning, I decided to bag Mero's trainers up with the rest of his clothes and put them away. When I walked into his room, I noticed there was a musty smell. It was coming from his defrosting hoodie. I picked up the bag and then spread his belongings on the floor, getting ready to place them in the hoover bag and then seal it shut. I took out his trainers and my hands started shaking. I held on tight to them, taking deep breaths and I closed my eyes, so I didn't have to see the blood on them. As I placed them in the bag, I kept asking myself, *why, why my baby?* I lifted his black shorts and pants, which had been cut because he had been stabbed in his legs. My breathing became laboured as I relived the whole episode again. Tears filled my eyes, and I began to cry. I felt so numb as I sat on the floor with Mero's belongings around me. I slowly finished packing his belongings away in the hoover bag, sealed it with grey tape, knowing they were his clothes from 9 September, and then put them away with the rest of his clothes.

For the rest of the day, I felt drained, and I spent the day in my bedroom, lying on my bed listening to music. Even though I was glad that I had all of Mero's belongings back with me, it still broke my heart into a thousand pieces. My chest was hurting and my anxiety was going through the roof, and I worked hard to calm myself down. Whenever I feel like this I just stay in my bedroom; it's my way of dealing with a bad day, and it's where I can be alone and gather my thoughts. Everyone around me thinks I am so strong, but sometimes I just want to be in someone's arms, and feel like they have got me, and where I can just cry, instead of me dealing with it on my own. I may have friends and family around me, but no one I can honestly say I can cry in their arms instead of having to be strong. At times I don't think I'd ever stop crying if I did have that special hug.

Chapter Eighteen

On the morning of 25 August, I met Hayley and Karla at St Kentigern's to dress the room. Rob was providing the table covers and he delivered them as well as helped put them on the tables. I borrowed the centre pieces, which were beautiful arrangements of flowers from my sister's company. We had blue runners on the tables topped off with sprinkles of diamonds, and on the stage, we had banners with Mero's World printed on them. We placed the raffle prizes on a table on the stage and we also had a table displaying a bleed cabinet, as well as a photo montage provided by Hayley of all of the things we'd achieved in our first year.

When we'd finished, I went to get my make-up done for the evening. After that I went home and relaxed for a couple of hours. I put my hair up in a bun and chose to wear a multi-coloured dress with beige heels. Remi and I were the first to arrive at the venue, followed by Karla and Jo. The deejay, Tromain, arrived and set up, and finally family and friends started to arrive. We had security on the door because it was a ticket-only event. I was sitting at a table with Jo, Caroline, Gaynor, Claire, Cloreece, Paula, Deanne, Naomi, Remi, Sadie and Caerus, my grandson. People who I worked with also turned up, Kerry, Jacqui, Saira, Ellen. Karla and her Uncle Allan, and Auntie Roma and their families came. Remi's god father, Shak, and Nicola, and Vicky came. Even Jamal, Remi's friend, came to show his support. They had been friends since they were five years old.

Quinton drove from Northampton and was staying in Manchester for the night. Frank, Sarah, Makala, Matthew, Kyle, and Josh, and not to mention Justina and the girls I went to Portugal with all came to show their support.

The room was filled with so much love and support, and I was grateful for everyone coming, and I especially enjoyed the many compliments I received about my dress. Remi and I took a photo next to the bleed cabinet, and I held a picture of Mero, in whose memory this had all come about. We then opened the buffet. There was a variety of food to eat, from sandwiches, chicken salad, pasta, fish, and other nibbles. Once the food was eaten, Quinton got on the stage and announced he was going to do the raffle. He called for me to read out the numbers, but I told him to get on with it. He made it fun, making everyone laugh by mc-ing on the mic. My sister and Pheobe helped by calling out the numbers, while I got up and wandered around the room, thanking everyone for coming and showing their support. A little later we all went outside to let off the fireworks. It was a cold and wet night. I didn't have a coat, so Matthew lent me his, and then went to let off the fireworks with Shak.

Since Mero's death I become emotional looking up to the sky and watching the fireworks go off. We went back inside when the display had finished, and my grandson Caerus took the mic from the deejay and was making funny noises, making everyone laugh. At one point he climbed on the stage and did a little dance, and then he bowed at the end. He is just the cutest! Quinton said it was time for me to give a speech, so I took the mic and kept it short and sweet.

I thanked everyone for coming, and all of the trustees - Deanne, Hayley, Jade, Gaynor and Neffie - for their support in helping with the charity grow from strength to strength. I especially thanked Karla, who had been a huge help in putting the evening together, and for the last song of the evening, the deejay played 'Baby Boy', the only song I play for Mero. I walked over to his picture and picked it up and sang to it, while Deanne picked up the board with the montage, showing all our achievements. Deanne and I were the only ones on the floor, while our guests stood at the edge of the dance floor and watched us dance. When the song ended, I held up Mero's photo and shouted, 'Mero's World!' and then I kissed the picture.

The evening came to an end, and we all packed up once the guests had gone. Deanne asked if we wanted to go back to her house to continue the celebrations. Deanne's son's dad was outside waiting for her and I climbed in his car and told him I was coming home with them. Paula, Quinton, Toni, Jo, Karla, Pheobe, Neffie, Tari, Jade and Ruth got taxis to Deanne's house. We carried on partying, and then I decided to leave because I was tired after such a long day. I took an Uber and when I got home, I showered and went straight to bed. The next morning I phoned my sister to ask if she could take me to St Kent's, where I left my car, and when she arrived, I told her over a cup of tea that I didn't know where Remi was, and that I was worried. She told me not to worry, as he was probably staying at Deanne's. It was while I was on the phone to Karla, asking if she'd seen Remi, that I heard a noise coming from upstairs. I laughed and explained to Karla it was Remi who was

144

in bed, and I made a note to myself to check his room first before I start telling people I don't know where he is!

I went to the cemetery to see Mero once I collected my car. I go every week and take him a purple rose. I didn't stay long, as it was cold and wet. On the drive home I started thinking, noticing how far we had come as a charity. Mero's legacy is living on, saving countless lives, and helping so many people through the work we do. My life had changed forever within the blink of an eye, and now I know with certainty that this is my new purpose in life. I had another hurdle ahead of me: Mero's two-year anniversary. I feel that's all my life is about now, just jumping over hurdles that keep coming up. On the morning of 9 of September 2023, I threw on a tracksuit and went to Rodgers the Florist on Princess Road and asked if they could make up two bouquets of flowers for me. All the women know me in there as I go every week, and I was well looked after. They created two beautiful bouquets of purple and white flowers. I went home and got dressed. We were all meeting at the cemetery at three o'clock. I chose to wear a multi-coloured summer dress, with gold and black sandals, and put my hair up in a bun. I waited for Remi to finish dressing and then picked my friend Nicola up on the way to Norton Street.

We had the car windows down and played music as we pulled up outside Mero's mural. I placed a bouquet of flowers on the pavement. Remi said that he wanted to go, and I asked Nicola if she would take a photo of us first, and we stood arm in arm looking at the mural. Next, we went to the cemetery. Remi took my car and went home, while Nicola and I went to the balloon shop and bought some purple balloons, as well as a large M and W for Mero's World to release later. I met Emma who is the mum of Hayden one of Mero's good friends. He used to stay at Hayden's house most weekends. She was buying some flowers for Mero's grave, and we walked back to the grave together. Remi had returned by this time, and we laid the bouquet on the grave. It was a hot day. Remi stayed in the car because it was so hot, and as we sat at the grave, we had a shot of brandy for Mero. My sister, D'margio, Paige, Damien, Chace, Neffie, Tari, Nubia, Mo, Reign, D'neay, my cousin Claire, Karla, Jo and Sarah, and Sadie and Caerus arrived, followed by Mero's friends. I gave everyone a shot of brandy for Mero, and Jamal opened his boot, which was filled with water and drinks, which I thought was so thoughtful of him. I played 'Baby Boy', blasting it out, and we then released the balloons. Claire shouted, 'Whose world is it?' and everyone replied, 'Mero's world,' but it was too quiet, and I said the response was so rubbish. I invited everyone back to mine for food and drinks and we all piled in the cars and left the cemetery.

It was a wonderful day. We were in the garden chilling and listening to music. Mero's and Remi's friends were also with us. We let off the purple flares and then had some food. Earlier I had made rum jelly shots to have at six thirty-six, the time I will never forget as it was the time Mero passed away. I handed out the shots and D'mornae filmed us on her camera, and we all shouted 'Mero!' People were struggling to get the jelly out and we all laughed. My cousins turned up, as well as Matthew, Kyle and Josh. I showed them where the food was and went back outside to be with my guests. I was feeling a little tipsy and I was able to smile without feeling guilty. For a while I used to feel guilty if I found myself laughing or smiling, or even having fun. I used to say to myself, *how can you have fun when your child isn't here?* It was getting dark, but still warm, and Matthew and Kyle let the fireworks off. People started leaving, but we stayed outside chatting until after midnight. Remi and Paula helped me clear up, and then we went to bed.

I had Mero's nineteenth birthday to sort out and the family were asking me what I was doing for it. I was unsure. I knew I didn't want another party at my house, so I decided on going to an all-you-can-eat buffet in town called Cosmo. I booked a table for immediate family at six o'clock to give people enough time to finish work and to get over there. On the morning of 20 September 2023, I woke up with mixed emotions. My baby turned nineteen and he wasn't even here. I sat on the sofa with a cup of tea, wondering what he would be like now, how deep would his voice be, how much facial hair he would have. I had all these questions running through my mind. Once I was dressed, I drove to the balloon shop and bought a large '19' balloon, as well as three small ones saying, 'Happy Birthday'. I already had birthday banners. I then went to the cemetery to decorate his grave. I wished him a happy birthday, and cried while I listened to music, I was playing for him, and I stayed for an hour and then went home.

For the rest of the day, I stayed at home, until it was time to pick up my grandson. We both got ready and drove to my sister's house. Remi was meeting us at the restaurant because he was at the cemetery with Jamal. The city centre was busy, and Damien was becoming frustrated with the heavy traffic and road closures. We finally arrived to find Remi, Neffie, Tari, Nubia, and others waiting for us. We were shown to our table, and I placed a framed picture of Mero on the table. The waitress came to take payment before we ate, but didn't take anything from me, Sadie and Remi. I smiled and said, 'Thank you, son,' as he mustn't have wanted us to pay.

As I was coming back to our table, Neffie was talking to a woman who said how sorry she was for my loss and mentioned that her daughter's grave is a few graves away from Mero's, and I said how sorry I was for her loss too. We all tried the different variety of foods on offer. I wasn't particularly keen on most of it and only had a few small plates. Before we left, we asked the waitress to take a picture of us all together. I had to leave a little earlier than I planned, because Sadie had to leave and Caerus got upset, and when Caerus wants to go, we must go. I was driven back to Naomi's where I collected my car, and then drove home with Caerus. It's after we have family gatherings, I sometimes sit there in disbelief that Mero isn't here and that he's missing out on so much. It's hard to take in, but I know for sure he is with us all in spirit, walking beside me every day.

One day I looked at my phone and noticed a missed call from Duane, Errol's brother. I then received a call from Gaynor telling me that Duane was trying to get hold of me. I phoned Duane and he went on to say that he was at the cemetery doing the rounds visiting the graves of family members. I paused and then asked him what's happened to Mero's grave. It wasn't the first time that something had happened to it; on two other occasions, someone has trashed his resting place, thrown his flowers, and breaking all of the things around it. He told me that someone had broken the head stone. I put the phone down and went to tell Remi. I had to wait for him to get dressed and we then drove to the cemetery. While we were on our way, Keena phoned me. She was at Mero's grave. I told her I was on my way. When we pulled up on the grass next to his grave, Keena was trying her best to clean up the mess.

Mero's headstone stands out from the rest of the other stones. I designed it myself. When we were looking at sample headstones, Remi said he wanted Mero's to be different because he was young. So, I drew a picture of how I wanted it to look and asked a head stone company to design it for me. It was in the shape of a giant letter R, with a love heart next to it and with his picture inside the love heart. There was also a small letter W on the top of the heart, to resemble a crown. Lastly, there was a pathway at the bottom with blue stone either side of it. Remi and I got out of the car, and as we walked towards the grave, I could see the worried expression on Keena's face. Looking at Mero's resting place, I just couldn't believe it. The flowers and stones were thrown everywhere, the Buddha statue I had placed on the grave was broken into pieces, and a wreath of flowers at the bottom of the grave had been destroyed. The letter

W was broken off in two different places and there were six marks on the headstone. Keena hugged me and told me how sorry she was. Remi then said, 'Mum, you've been this strong up to now, don't let this break you.' I looked at them both, and said, 'My boy's gone, this is just material stuff.' Deep down I was so hurt and angry, wondering who would stoop so low to trash someone else's resting place. It's like I haven't suffered enough. I began to question myself, asking myself what I had done to deserve all of this pain I was going through.

We cleaned the grave up, having to throw away everything. It looked so bare when we finished, and I said to Remi that I wished I could get it remade and put in our garden at home. I then got in touch with Southern Cemetery, asking them if there was anything they could do. There wasn't and there weren't any CCTV cameras installed either. I originally contacted the company who had designed the headstone for us to see if it was insured. I mustn't have been in the right frame of mind when it was commissioned because I didn't take out insurance. I then emailed a picture of the headstone to James Hilton on Barlow Moor Road in Chorlton, asking if they could fix it. They replied that they could fix it, and that it was going to cost £1,500, with £179.00 added on to insure it. I just agreed, as it needed fixing. I both hated and felt disheartened going to the cemetery and seeing it like that. With the help from family, we were able to restore the headstone to its former self. I still kept asking myself why I was being hurt in so many ways, when I had lost my child in such cruel circumstances. I realised materialistic things didn't mean anything to me anymore, they weren't important; life is, and we only get one shot at it, and we don't know when it's our time to go, so we have to live each day as if it's our last.

Chapter Nineteen

I was asked to do a short clip before the awards ceremony, because I was one of the finalists. It was about the charity and the work I had done in memory of Mero. I met a reporter at Norton Street where she filmed me talking in front of Mero's mural. I found the perfect dress; it was long and black, fitted at the waist with a long slit down the side, and it had golden embroidery around the neckline. I had my make-up done, and Sadie put my hair up for me. I was given three additional tickets, so I invited Naomi, Karla and Gaynor along for support. The ceremony was being held at the monastery in Gorton. We all met at my house and Naomi drove us there. Gaynor had chosen a beautiful multi-coloured dress, while Karla wore a black fitted dress, and Naomi chose to wear white. We were all excited when we arrived at the monastery; there was a photographer waiting to take our picture in front of the BBC backdrop. We were then given a glass of Prosecco, and we sat in the reception area and waited for the other guests to arrive.

We were told we could go into the room where the ceremony was being held. I checked the seating plan; we were going to be sitting at table six. As soon as I entered the room, I was mesmerised by the décor; the whole room was lit up in purple, and straight away I said it was a sign from Mero. Before the evening started, we took pictures on our phones of us walking down the long runway with the purple lights. It was a sign from my boy; everywhere was purple. When we returned to our table, I took a picture of Mero out and placed it on the table in front of me. This was going to be the first year the BBC Radio Awards had added the category of bravery. A family friend Akiem and his parents were sitting at the table in front of us. His mum Hilary turned round and asked Gaynor if Errol supported me in what I was doing, and Gaynor replied, 'No, he doesn't.' Akiem was there to present the winner with their award from another category. I gave him and his mum a hug. Hilary was a good friend of Mero's nana, Eldora.

We had a meal consisting of chicken breast, roast potatoes and veg, with gravy. It was well presented, and I had chocolate cake with strawberry ice cream for my desert, decorated with popcorn. The food was delicious and when we had finished, it was cleared away and the ceremony began. It was hosted by Anna Jameson. She started by getting everyone in the room to stand up and then took a selfie on her phone, with us in the background. There were a few awards before the category I had been nominated for, and the butterflies began to stir in my stomach. My wait was finally over. On the big screen, we were shown the short clips of the finalists. I was up against Darren Buckley and a few other amazing people. Darren and I kept in touch after the awards and follow each other on Facebook. Naomi began to cry when she saw me on the big screen, because she was so nervous.

When all of the clips had been shown, the judge came on the screen and apologised for why he couldn't be there in person. He then went on to say that he had picked this person due to the personal tragedy they had been through, and how they had turned things around to help others and save lives. Then I heard my name, Kelly Brown. I looked up at the big screen and saw my name on it with 'Winner', above it. My friends at the table congratulated me. I nudged Naomi and told her she was coming on the stage with me, and we made our way through the audience who were clapping loudly. We got on to the stage and Anna gave me a hug and said, 'Well done.' I was holding on to Mero's picture tightly. Anna said she was sorry for what I had been through, and asked if I would like to say something. I said I was honoured, and I held up the picture of Mero and said that he was with me every step of the way, helping me to make a change in this cruel world we live in. I was presented with my award, while having my rock, Naomi, standing by my side.

We walked off the stage and through a door to do an interview with two reporters. One held the camera and filmed us, while the other asked me how I felt winning the Bravery Award. I looked at the camera and said it was an honour, I was just blown away with it all. After losing Mero, I wanted to make a change. I know everyone's journeys are different, and every parent who loses a child goes through their own journey. Mine was to fight. I had a fight in my belly for change, and I turned that fight into change, and I will continue doing it until Greater Manchester is a safer place for the next generation. Children of Years Five and Six are a vital age to educate before they enter high school. They're at the important age where we need to get through to them and say, 'Look, don't go down that path, it's not worth it.'

Once the interview was over, we went back to our table. Hilary and Akiem hugged me and congratulated me. As I sat down, I couldn't believe that I had won another award. I messaged Remi to tell him that I had won, and I kept staring at Mero's picture, feeling overwhelmed. Naomi and I went to the bar and ordered a brandy and Coke. Karla had messaged our friends to let them know I had won. Towards the end of the night Anna called all of the winners to the stage to take a picture together. The audience got out of their seats to take photos too. I was smiling from ear to ear. It was an amazing end to a beautiful night. Naomi dropped us back at my house, where we had a cup of tea, and I took a photo of the award and made a post on Facebook, letting all of Mero's followers know that I had won the award, which I placed in the cabinet alongside the other two awards I had won earlier in the year.

My phone was pinging with well-wishing messages from Facebook and Instagram. I still didn't know who had nominated me for the award, until I saw a message on Facebook from a girl I didn't know, who was saying she was glad that she had nominated me and thought that I deserved to win out of everybody else who had been nominated. I was blown away that someone who didn't know me personally had nominated me because she had seen all the hard work I had been doing in the community and schools, and more importantly for the kids. That night I went to bed with the biggest smile on my face, feeling equally happy that I had won the award two days after my angel's birthday.

The decision was taken to move the Youth Hub from the library to the Methodist Church, which is situated on the corner of Platt Lane and Hart Road. We'd been at the library for over a year, but the church was free on the day we wanted, which was Tuesday evenings, instead of Friday evening. This worked better for me, Karla and Natasha, who also runs the club with me. Since the move, we've managed to bring in different age groups, ranging from seven to sixteen, and fifteen to twenty kids come on a weekly basis. I received an email from Gavin Evan asking if the children would like to take part in spray painting a mural down one of the alleyways that leads to the Aldi supermarket. I sent a reply thanking him for wanting to include the Youth Hub in something so positive in Fallowfield. When I told the children they were excited to be involved in the project. The following Saturday I arranged with Natasha to meet the children - Ben, Reece, Keziah, Kylah, Shay, Poppy, Lillie, Harrison, Finleigh, and Pheobe - outside the Methodist Church. I'd asked the parents and carers for their permission earlier and asked that the children be collected at three o'clock.

We met Oskar in the alleyway, and on the wall was the outline of a heart shape and the words 'We love Fallowfield' inside it. The children gathered round Oskar, and he told them what they were going to do and the importance of them wearing protective clothing and masks. When they were kitted out, Oskar showed them how to use the spray paints. They were only going to use the colours of red, yellow, and orange to fill in the mural, and me being a big kid myself, I joined in them. Natasha took pictures, and we all had fun. We had a short break so the kids could use the toilet and have a snack, and then we went back to work. Oskar showed the children how to use different shapes to create different patterns, which the children loved. However, they loved it even more when Oskar said they could spray paint their names on the mural. Reece commented that people could see who had done the mural, and they happily painted their names. I stood on a stool and painted my signature, which is 'Mero's World', at the top.

The children had done an amazing job, and Oskar said he would go over the outline of the mural to make it stand out. Some of the parents came to see the mural. The kids were proud and excited to show their parents what they had been doing. People who were passing through the alleyway commented positively on what we were doing, and when we had finished, we cleared the alleyway up and left Oskar to finish outlining the mural. Later that night Oskar messaged me, saying the group of kids he'd worked with that afternoon were the best group that year. He also sent a copy of the finished mural, which I posted on the Mero's World Facebook page. Oskar had signed his signature in the bottom right-hand corner, and I felt proud and happy being a part of the project, especially doing it for Fallowfield, the area that holds a special place in my heart, and the area that Mero loved.

Chapter Twenty

For the Youth Hub to have potential and grow organically, I needed to apply to various organisations for funding. It was all very new to me, and I struggled to get my head around it all. I got in touch with a friend, Madeeha, who has experience in filling in funding forms, and she suggested that we approach the National Lottery for funding. It took us approximately a week to fill in the forms. We were asking for funding to run the Youth Hub for five years. Once we submitted the form we had to wait for a response. About a week later, I received an email to say we hadn't been successful. I refused to let it deflate me and I got in touch with MACC. They are Manchester's local voluntary and community sector support organisation, and I asked if someone there could help me with the funding forms.

I was advised to apply to the Lottery Community Fund for up to £20k. I did some research and discovered that funders like to see charities start off with small funding pots to show that they can manage the funds efficiently and grow bigger. So Madeeha and I applied for a smaller pot of money. They got back to me and asked to see the charity's bank statements. I knew from then we were going to be accepted. As soon as I sent the statements off, I received an email thanking me for my quick response, and then later received another email from the Lottery saying they were going to fund our Youth Hub. I was over the moon with this news, because it meant we could provide the children of the community a stable and safe place.

As I continued to push for more resources and for the charity to grow, I saw on the news that the government were banning machetes and zombie knives. From this I was approached by *BBC Northwest Tonight*, BBC Radio, Hits Radio and *The Manchester Evening News* to give my thoughts on the subject. In my interview I stated that I was finally happy it had happened, but it shouldn't be taking eight months for the ban to be put in place, as they banned XL bully dogs within three months. This led me to wonder if the government were really bothered at all about our children's lives. My interviews were shown across all levels of the media, which made me realise I had reached a point now where I was not shy in getting my point of view across to anyone from the media.

I was reading the interview I had given online. I was satisfied with what I had to say, and then I started reading the online comments. I came across one comment, which was obviously from a troll, who said: 'Ha ha look at all the white people sticking together.' I wanted to post a reply to the comment but thought against it. I reasoned that there are some shallow people in this world, and furthermore, he had looked at my picture, thinking that I was a white woman and little did he know that I'm of white and African origin, and proud of it. What it says to me, is that you can't judge a book by its cover. The post centred around three murders that had happened in Nottingham of white victims, which was committed by a black man. I've learned over time not to focus on negative people and things. I chose instead, to focus on my network of amazing and supportive people I have around me, who follow Mero on social platforms, who support us in everything we do, as we grow as a charity.

I've always wanted to do an opening ceremony, and I got my chance when a contemporary statue called the Knife Angel made up of 100,000 knives, created by Alfie Bradley and the British Ironworks Centre based in Oswestry, came to Bury. I first heard about it after Mero passed away, and when it came to Blackburn, I went to see it with Gaynor and D'mornae, and I brought a photo of Mero with me to leave at the site. Looking up at the statue, I could see it was both very powerful and emotional. It seemed to me the angel was holding its hands out and asking the question *Why? Why have all of these lives been taken by a knife?* I received a text from Roy, who I have been working closely with running knife crime workshops throughout Manchester. In his text, it said the Knife Angel is coming to Bury, would I do a speech at the opening ceremony? I messaged him back straightaway that I would be honoured to do it. We have done so much work in Bury around knife crime, and there is now a Mero's World bleed cabinet installed there too.

I have created a good network around me, and I have supportive connections made up of MPs councillors, and the Violence Reduction Unit, who have had a positive impact on the Mero's World team and what we wish to achieve. Afzal Khan, the MP for the Gorton, Fallowfield and Levenshulme areas has been supportive from the beginning. He can see the passion and drive I have for change around knife crime. His PA, Tom, contacted me and told me Afzal was standing up in the House of Commons to talk about me and my fight in Manchester, installing bleed cabinets and running the Youth Hub, and also to share my story to prevent another parent from going through loss from knife crime. He asked the Minister for Crime and Policing, Chris Philp, if he would meet me on record. He agreed and once again I was approached by Hits Radio for an interview, and my friend Keena sent me an article from *The Manchester Evening News*, reporting that a minister was going to meet a campaigning mum of a murdered teen chased down and stabbed. I stressed that the minister needs to sit in a room with some mothers who have lost their child to knife crime, and to hear our stories. I was more than happy that he agreed to meet me.

On the same day I received an email from the Legends of Industry Awards, to say that I had been nominated for an award recognising my work in supporting and saving the lives of young adults in the community. I was screaming and dancing around my bedroom, and I kept on reading the email in disbelief that I had won another award. I was truly blown away with this award, which will be presented at a black-tie event on Thursday 26 September 2024 at The Hilton Hotel in Manchester. I'm going to have to find another black dress, which I'm not complaining about! When I sit and think about how many awards Mero's World charity has won, it's out of this world. *How many awards does my baby boy want me to win?* I ask myself. I give thanks every day to him for giving me the strength to get up and fight. I go to bed at night and always talk to him, asking him, '*What's next,* son?' And I'm not joking when I say there is something from the Youth Hub to support families. It's all about prevention and saving lives, and more importantly providing a safe place for the children.

The day had finally arrived when I was going to do a speech at the Knife Angel opening ceremony in Bury. I wore a hoodie with Mero's picture on it, and my friend Jen and her cousin had knitted 20 purple hearts. Jen is the lady I did a house exchange with, and we've kept in touch ever since. The rain was coming down heavily. I never let any type of weather stop me from doing things. Earlier I'd received a text from Jennifer, saying, 'Jeez, have you seen the weather?' I messaged back, saying: 'I know.' Jennifer, Gaynor and Nicola were coming with me, so I picked up Gaynor first, who had texted me asking where I was. I laughed and said she was impatient, and that I was around the corner. From Gaynor's I picked up Nicola. I had the heating on full blast, it was so cold. Jennifer was next and we set off for Bury, I introduced Jennifer to Nicola and Gaynor, it was her first time meeting them, but she has heard so much about them because she has been editing my book. Jennifer said it was nice to put a face to the name. We had such a giggle driving to Bury, where we talked about all sorts of things, namely me having the heat turned up high and Gaynor overheating!

After parking the car, we walked through the town centre. We had to ask a security guard where the Knife Angel was, and he pointed us in the right direction. When I looked at the powerful piece of artwork, it was as if with its hands outstretched, it was asking why. It was cold, so we went to find a café. As I approached a girl to ask where the nearest café was, she said, 'You're Mero's mum, aren't you?' She had gone to school with Mero. She hugged me, and said she had noticed me earlier, because she had seen my hoodie. Gaynor knew the girl's mum, and we hugged again, and we left for a café where we could have a hot drink to keep warm.

When we went back to the statue, Roy met us with a joke; that's Roy for you. He introduced me to Simone from BBC Radio, who wanted to do an interview. Karl, was also there, he and I do workshops together. Sandra Walmsley, the Mayor of Bury spoke to me, and we had a picture together in front of the sculpture. Sandra asked me if I had just won an award at Gorton Monastery. I replied I had, and she said that's where she recognised me from. I was then introduced to some people from Bury Council and others who were supporting the event. Before the start, I did an interview with Simone, and it took place under a gazebo. She asked me to say my name, and then it started. 'Mero's World came about after I lost my son in 2021. He was a victim of knife crime. We are now a registered charity, and we install bleed cabinets over Greater Manchester. We have opened a Youth Hub in Fallowfield, and I support other parents who have also gone through the loss of a child, as well as go into schools and PRUs to raise awareness of knife crime.'

Simone asked what it feels like to see the Knife Angel. I replied that it was overwhelming and powerful at the same time. 'When I look at it, it's saying. "Why have all these lives been taken?" But it's an honour to be here in Bury today to represent the Knife Angel and to raise awareness around knife crime because it's not going to go away, and more needs to be done.' She then asked about the work we were doing to ensure more is done. She mentioned the bleed cabinet we installed in Old Trafford. Being an Old Trafford girl, she said it sent shock waves through the community, and that the work we were doing was amazing. I replied: 'I understand every mother's journey is different when losing a child, but two months after losing Mero I decided that I was not going to be one of those mums who sit down, but one who gets up and fights.' When asked what having the Knife Angel means to the community, I replied, 'I'm hoping it will raise awareness of knife crime and to show the youths, and general public, how powerful and important it is. Many people shy away from it until it happens to them, or on their doorstep, and we all have to pull together to make a change.'

Once my interview finished, Simone started the ceremony, introducing all of the other speakers. The rain was coming down and it was cold, and I stood under my umbrella waiting until it was my turn to speak. A grandmother read a poem she had written for her grandson who is in prison for killing someone with a knife. Her poem was powerful, and it showed the ripples that knife crime creates for families, as well as the perpetrator's families. Clive Knowles was one of the people who created the Knife Angel in the British Ironwork Centre. When he finished his speech I went over to say hello. I had met Clive over two years ago after he had reached out to me, and Gaynor and I went to the Centre to meet him. He told me about the Knife Angel and also about the

Manchester Bee, which was made up from knives and guns from Manchester.

It was my turn to give my speech, and Nicola took out her phone to film me, and that's when the nerves kicked in. I took a deep breath and started talking. 'Hi, my name is Kelly Brown. On the ninth of September 2021, my sixteen-year-old son was a victim of knife crime. The effect it has had on me is to destroy me, and it's been so hard on my family and friends, and even the community.' My mind went blank for a split second; it was one of the hardest speeches I've ever had to make. I looked at the people staring at me and other people who were walking past the statue. Someone from the crowd shouted, 'You can do it.' I apologised and carried on. I said, 'One careless act can ruin so many lives. It's like throwing a stone in a river and watching the ripples getting bigger and bigger. That's how many lives have been affected, even the perpetrators who have taken my son's life have now messed up their own lives and are serving life sentences. Since my son's death I have formed a charity called Mero's World Foundation, and we have been installing bleed cabinets over Greater Manchester. There are fifteen of them in Bury alone and with the help of my Bury family - they know who they are, Paddy, Tina, Roy, Karl, Graham and Wendy - we've also been delivering knife crime workshops and supporting families who have been affected by knife crime. Having the Knife Angel will help promote the consequences of knife crime and how it represents the victims and promotes social change not only to knife crime, but violent crime too. Thank you.'

My heart was racing all through my speech and I was grateful when it finished. Roy said I couldn't disappear now I had spoken; he said Clive had personalised achievement certificates for each of us. We were presented with our certificates and had our photographs taken. We headed back to the carpark, getting lost on the way, and finally then back in the car on the way back to Manchester. We were all cold and tired, and I had the car heater on keeping us all warm. I dropped Jennifer off first, then Gaynor, and Nicola and I went to Aldi, as she was cooking that night. My friends Karla and Sarah dropped by, and we spent a relaxing evening together. After that day I was mentally and physically drained. When I do talks, or I'm with friends, or driving, I find myself drifting, day dreaming, thinking about Mero and asking myself, *Is my son really not here with me?*

Most nights I wake up and watch videos of him on rewind, looking through my phone at pictures of him, with tears rolling down my cheeks, trying to be quiet so I don't disturb Remi sleeping in the other room. One thing I can take from this journey that I'm on is that people I've known since I was young haven't been there for me, and people who I've recently met have supported me in ways I've never experienced before. My good friend Matthew, he has faith in me and what I want to achieve in helping others. He believes in me and that means a lot to me. The support and guidance I've received from him makes me feel like I've known him all my life.

Chapter Twenty-One

Monday 8 April, I was meeting with Chantel Miller, lead investigator, and Sophie Mellor, case supervisor, from the IOPC at Longsight Library. We were meeting to receive their findings on the complaint I submitted in the way the police dealt with the run up to the two incidents that occurred in 2021 before Mero was killed. I met Sophie in the reception area, and we went to a back room where Chantel was waiting. We hugged and then sat down. Chantel asked how I'd been and how the awards ceremony went. I asked her which one, as I'd won three and have another one to collect in September. She was impressed as she handed me a copy of the report, and we looked at the main points, as it was a long report, and Chantel said I could read the rest when I got home.

Regarding the findings, the report found the officers did follow procedures when they visited my home on both occasions in 2021. We both agreed that they could have shown more empathy on both visits, and I had previously asked if I could speak to the officers in question face to face. They didn't/wouldn't agree to this, so Sophie asked if I would be happy to speak to someone else from the force. I replied that I would. Chantel then told me more training is being put in place to deal with reports like this. Throughout the report I noticed there was a lack of communication with all of the parties involved, and I intended to address this when I went to Westminster on 24 April.

An hour went by, and we went through all of the main points. Afterwards, Chantel advised me not to share it, and I joked that I would share it with everyone I knew. She then admitted that this case was disturbing and would stay with her for a long time. The outcome stated that nothing is going to be taken further, and I can say I was astounded by the lack of communication between the Youth Offending Team, the police and Social Services. More training needs to be provided, and communication needs to be tighter, so kids at risk don't fall through the gaps. After the meeting Chantel told me to keep up with the good work, but when I drove home I put the report away until I was in the right frame of mind to read it fully. On the whole, I felt deflated with the outcome, knowing it's not going to change anything, and it won't bring my baby boy back.

The big day finally arrived, and Hayley, one of the trustees and me were travelling to London to have a meeting with Chris Philp, minister of crime, policing and fire, and Afzal Khan MP at Westminster. Hits Radio announced that I was attending Westminster that day and would be interviewed after the meeting. I woke early and was excited and ready for the day ahead of me. I dressed in a grey pants suit, with a white top and black boots, and a long black overcoat. I ordered a taxi to take me to the station, forgetting it was going to be rush hour, which added to my anxiety, as I hate being late. Hayley sent me a message saying there had been a crash on the M60, and that if I got to the station before she did, then I was to get on the train and she would get a later one.

At this point I was feeling very nervous. I didn't want to miss the train, and I didn't want to go on my own. What didn't help was the taxi driver was driving slowly. Hayley phoned me and said she would get on at Stockport and sent me my ticket. I arrived at the station ten minutes before the train was due to leave. I messaged Hayley to say I was on the train, and she said she was at Stockport. I felt I could finally breathe knowing we would go to London together. Hayley is the trustee who set the charity up for me as well as the email address, and I'm forever texting her to say the password to the emails doesn't work.

When she got on the train, we both complimented each other on how smart we both looked. Hayley made the train journey go so quickly because she had me giggling all the way there. I gave Hayley the parliamentary debates to look at, which I had received from Afzal Khan's PA prior to the visit, and she laughed and said she had watched the full debate. We looked at the group chat I had set up with all of the trustees. She said she wouldn't want me to be her boss, and I laughed and said I'm okay, I just like things doing straight away, I hate having to wait for anything. I always say to myself the universe is teaching me patience. We finally arrived at London Euston and went to the toilets. I used the toilet and waited for Hayley outside, while she was waiting for me inside, thinking I was still in the cubicle. This sums us both up, and we looked at each other and burst out laughing. Hayley hadn't realised there was a timer when buying our tube tickets, and she kept running out of time, and wasn't able to buy our tickets. She hit her lip with her phone in frustration, and when we finally were on the Tube, I noticed she had a small lump where she'd hit her lip, and we burst out laughing.

I've never been on the Tube before; it was very warm and fast. I find in London everyone rushes about, and it's too fast for me. We got off the Tube and walked through Green Park, and Hayley said Buckingham Palace was just at the bottom. I have never been to the city area of London before, and it was the first time seeing the palace, and we took photos outside it. From Buckingham Palace, we then walked through St James's Park to get to parliament. It was a nice day; the sun was out, and it was fun to do some sightseeing along with the other tourists. Next, we went to Downing Street, where there were guards standing outside the building with guns. We took photos next to the guards on horses.

We were still early for the meeting, so we sat on the green outside Parliament, where it was busy and there was a heavy police presence. I took out a Mero's World t-shirt that I'd brought with me and laid it on the grass verge facing Big Ben and Hayley took a picture. I then held it up so the writing on the back saying *'Put down the knives, save all lives'* could be seen. After that we walked to the River Thames. At this point we could see the whole parliament, a helicopter flying overhead and the London Eye across the road. At the bottom of the road, we came to the Covid Wall, which was very powerful to see. It represented everyone who had lost their lives to Covid, and was filled with over 239,000 red love hearts with the names of the victims written inside.

It was coming up to two o'clock, so we headed to the side of parliament, and were confronted by a long line of people queuing. We joined the line and phoned Zainab, Afzal Khan's PA to let her know we were in the queue. She told us to meet them in the café once we were inside the building. I asked someone who was in front of us in the queue if it was always this busy, and they replied it wasn't, it was just there were other things happening that day. Overall we queued for at least an hour and a half and suffice it to say our feet were killing! We eventually reached the security point at three thirty. Our bags were searched and we were given a security badge. I phoned Zainab and she came down to meet us with another of Afzal Khan's PAs.

Zainab informed us our meeting was due to start at four o'clock, and she offered to show us round the building. Hayley and I looked at each other and said we'd prefer to go to the café. As we walked through the main hall, there were high ceilings and it was decorated beautifully, but very cold. Zainab told us that was where the Queen lay in state, and people queued for days to pay their respects. We passed through some large wooden doors and a security point, where the hallway was brightly lit. There were high arched ceilings, stained-glass windows and large pictures of memorials on the walls. Stone benches lined the length of the hallway with black padded cushions, and a large statue stood next to them. I asked Zainab if I could take a photograph, and she said I could in this section only. Walking through another set of wooden doors, we entered a large reception area with corridors leading off to other areas. Afzal met us and Hayley introduced herself. Zainab said we would have to walk back to the main entrance to meet Chris Philp's PA Hayley and I tried not to groan as our feet were still sore. Near the main doors we were met by three women, and they directed us to the office, which was in the outdoor area, which reminded me of a stone castle.

One of the PAs phoned the minister to let him know we had arrived, and after ten minutes we were shown into his office. It was nice and warm inside. There were tables and chairs and two comfy chairs, and the walls were plain beige. I shook the minister's hand and introduced myself as Kelly Brown, mother of Rhamero West. Hayley introduced herself and we sat down. The PAs were sitting at the desks taking notes, and then Afzal told me to start. I looked at Chris and told him I was going to share my story of the day I lost my baby boy, and then when I had finished, he said as a parent himself, he couldn't imagine what I had gone through. He then asked about the boys who'd murdered my son. I told him that they were all serving life in prison. He asked about their ages, and I replied they were 16, 18, 19 and 19 at the time. I told him of the charity we'd set up in memory of Mero, the Youth Hub we run, the mothers I support who've been through similar experiences, how I go into schools etc. to raise awareness of knife crime, and the ripple effects it has on the families, friends and the communities left behind. I then raised some points with him to which he replied.

Kelly:

- Banning knives needs to be given priority. It is clear the government can get things done when it needs to – e.g. banning XL bull dogs within three months – but the same priority isn't being given to knives.
- Fifty bleed cabinets have been installed across Greater Manchester. These need to be in schools as a precautionary measure. Kits for schools' cost £100 and a full bleed cabinet costs £480.
- There is a lack of trauma-informed support or counselling for young people whose friends have been killed by knife crime, alongside a lack of youth hubs where young people can go to socialise and stay off the streets.
- Preventative measures and education need to start at the end of primary school. In Years Five and Six, young people already know about knife crime and are finding knives on the street. Behavioural issues at this age only go on to escalate without intervention.

The minister:

- Ban on sale, possession, manufacture of zombie knives will come into force September 2024. There is a delay because there is a process/scheme for people to forfeit their knives which are currently legal, but which will become illegal by September 2024.
- In September 2024 police will also be getting a new power whereby if they have a warrant to search someone's property for something

else and they find lots of knives (even legal ones) that they think will be used for crime, these can be confiscated.

- Government is funding VRUs to provide this youth provision/support/interventions. Funding for VRUs will be doubled next year to £25M.

- The Youth Endowment Fund is working on developing analytics which will identify 50 - 100 young people in each local authority who are at risk of going into serious crime and try to intervene. Interventions will include Cognitive Behaviour Therapy, mentoring and diversion tactics. Currently, indicators are being developed for this, including school safeguarding referrals, social service notes, mental health referrals.

- Stop and search is effective at getting knives off the street. The Home Office is investing in technology in the form of handheld devices for police officers to scan big crowds of people at a distance for knives (it will be able to differentiate between knives and keys, for example.) This allows police to scan big crowds of people quickly and easily without the use of stop and search. This technology is 12 - 18 months away.

ACTION:

- Minister Philp's office to look into how they can provide bleed kits more widely as a government. This is currently the responsibility of the Department for Health and Social Care (alongside defibrillators) so they will speak to DHSC colleagues about how these can be rolled out more widely. There is currently a DHSC pilot being run with the National Police Chiefs Council on bleed kits so will look at how this is going. He will also consider how VRUs can deploy bleed kits more consistently.

ACTION:
- Minister Philp to write to the Schools Minister about prevention and first aid education in schools.
- He will highlight the need to talk to Years Five and Six about knife crime and encourage more first aid provision in schools which includes how to stem bleeds.
- Afzal:
- Greater Manchester Police have told Afzal about problems with scanning knives that are brought online and delivered through the post, via some courier services, which aren't scanned so reach the buyer. Whereas other postal services identify these in scanning and screen them.

ACTION:
- Afzal to find out more details of this issue and share with Minister Philp.

With the time we had to address the issues, I found that the meeting was a positive one moving forward. Chris thanked us for coming and we all took a photograph together. One of the PAs said she would be in touch with us around the bleed cabinets. When we left the Minister's office Afzal, Hayley and I took a photograph outside Big Ben before leaving parliament.

Next, we met Georgia, who worked for Hits Radio for our interview. It took place on grass in a quiet area near parliament. I spoke about some of the points we discussed in the meeting with the minister, and Hayley added how she thought it had been a positive meeting. At the end, Georgia asked me how she felt Mero would be feeling now looking down at his mum. I replied he would be bursting with pride, saying, *That's my mum.* We walked to the River Thames and there we said goodbye to Georgia. Hayley looked at me and admitted that she had been holding back her tears in the meeting. I asked her why. She said she knew all about my story, and it's the fact of where I am now; having a meeting in parliament because of the loss of Rhamero. 'Look how far you've come. Who would have ever thought you'd be in parliament addressing knife crime and sharing your story?'

Before we got on the Tube, we both put on our Mero's World t-shirts and took a photograph with parliament in the background. We didn't have to walk far to the Tube station, because it was just across the road. When we arrived at Euston, we had two hours before our train departed. There was a Nando's close, so we decided to have dinner. We had a well-deserved glass of wine with our food and toasted to the day we'd had. It was a relief finally to get on the train and sit in our seats. It had been a long day and we felt exhausted from all of the walking we'd done. On the journey back I put the meeting with the minister on social media, and then put my headphones on and slept.

When we arrived in Stockport, we both decided to get off the train and take Ubers home. I got home at eleven o'clock, showered and got into bed. I messaged Remi, asking where he was, and he asked how the visit went and said he was proud of me and that my voice was being heard. I fell asleep straight away, but I woke at three o'clock. It was one of those nights where I wasn't able to sleep through. I started thinking about where I'd just been, taking it all in as I lay in bed watching one of Mero's videos on repeat, listening to Paloma Faith's 'only love can hurt like this'.

I'm doing all of this and fighting for a change because of the loss of my precious boy. It's almost three years since Mero left us and I still keep a bedroom for him. I suppose that's my way of holding on to him even though he is no longer with us. Grief comes and hits you in different ways, and this is my way of coping. I will continue with the charity, the Youth Hub, and the workshops, as long as there is a need to highlight the devastating effects of knife crime.

My journey has also taught me that it's okay not to be okay, and to show my emotions. Now that I've lost my son, I've gained a voice I never knew existed. I'm now a mother on a mission for a change, and that's to have our own building for Mero's World Youth Hub, which will also have a support network, with mental health and trauma support for children who have lost friends in a violent manner. There will be mentors to guide them, and for society to believe in them and to help them achieve a better future. We will be installing more bleed cabinets, not just in Greater Manchester, but nationwide and in schools, and most importantly going into more schools across the country to do more advocacy work. I'm also looking forward to receiving the Legend of Industry award in September.

The next day, I woke up to everyone messaging me and replying to my posts about me being at Westminster.

'Inspirational u are Kell' - Tracie Jones

'You are so inspirational' - Laurz Cully

'Doing Manchester and all families proud' - Avril Gormley

'Well done, Kelly, your boy will be looking down, thinking that's my mum' - Jean Wilson

'100% behind you, Mero's World to be the voice for us mothers and sons' - Nicola Dylan Wardle

'My idol, so proud of you Kel, truly an inspiration and Mero is holding your hand every step of the way. I want to say a huge thank you for really taking your pain and turning it into determination to make a change for our babies' - Chelsea Devaney

'You're an amazing, strong woman, even through your pain you're helping other young people keep going and stay strong' - Jane Hutton

'Amazing Kelly, so proud of you, queen' - Kelly Browne

'So determined, you achieve everything you set out to do, you are incredible' - Pam Whittle

'You are an inspiration. Well done darling, you're doing all us mothers proud and also your family and sons' - Chelsea Harvey

Acknowledgements

Firstly, I would like to thank my son Remi for being my biggest supporter, and never leaving my side through all of this, I love you with all my heart.

My beautiful angel Mero, for giving me the strength and guidance to achieve all that I have in his memory, so far, and in helping others.

My precious grandson, Caerus, for being my little saver. When my days were dark, he would brighten them up for me.

My sister, Naomi, for being my rock, my best friend, my soul mate and for always being there for me. To my family, thank you and I love you all.

My trustees: Deanne, Jade, Neffie, Hayley, Gaynor. I couldn't have come this far without help from you.

Ruby for designing the front cover of the book, and Jennifer - without you having faith and pushing me, this book wouldn't have come to life, so thank you for believing I could do it.

Thanks to Matthew and Keena, and lastly to Frank, Kirstie, Paula, Karla, Nicola, Jo, and Sarah for not leaving my side, and for all your continued support.

Awards won:
Pride of Manchester
Creating Safer Neighbourhoods
Manchester BBC Radio Bravery Awards
And in September – The Legend of Industry Awards

In Loving Memory of Rhamero Latteece West
9/9/2004 to 9/9/2021

Mero's Poem

If you knew of the place that collected my tears, you
would literally drown in my sorrows, entangled in
fear, but reaching out for hope you'd found your
tomorrows. But I'm feeling weighed down and
swimming in the deep end, whilst holding on to
memories and desperate to keep them washed away
by the waves towards the depths of the ocean.
Searching for the words that were left unspoken. It
feels like I screamed but I never made the noise, I
don't want to come back without my baby boy. I
wonder if he sees me, or if he heard me pass. I
wonder if he's looking for my purple heart. I wonder if
he's looking at the same part of the sky, wandering
the clouds, looking down and asking me why.
I would hold him close with everything left in me, and
say, I know you should have grown into the rest of
your destiny. Mero, you were the best of me, and
sometimes it feels like you're right here next to me.
All the darkness in the world couldn't dim your light.
We painted the sun for you, son. So, you'll always
shine, we wrapped it around the branches of the
family tree.
Where we live in a space between dreams and
reality. When you passed, I never knew where you
passed. I never knew where butterflies went, but
since you've been gone, I always seem to find them.
Are they angels with wings, searching for their
halos? Is it you that always seems to paint the
skylines with rainbows? If you're sending Mum a
sign, that's no less amazing, and you always seem to
do it on a special occasion. People won't understand,

they must think we never speak. But you talked to us all since we gathered on your seventeenth.
Rhamero, your voice will echo for eternity, and your friends and your family love you unreservedly.
Your pictures, your voice notes, we watch video on rewind, it's like we are pushing helplessly against the sands of time. The community united all because of you, and there are adults and children watering the roots.
That's because you walked in extraordinary shoes. And now we're moving mountains that they thought we'd never move.
You are the rings of Saturn; you are the particles that sparkle. No, you are the universe, you are everything remarkable.
I miss my little joker that left a mess in every room. You had a smile that was brighter than the surface of the moon.
When I see purple and I'm blue, it always cheers me up because it makes me think of you.
You made the house fun, it was different before, i remember your wet curls would be dripping on the floor.
I won't forget you, jumping out to scare me when I got in.
Or how you valued family time when you met up with your cousins.
I can see us walking in the park, I'd be talking to your daughter, and telling your wife to buy you strawberry water.
We'd laugh about how you were nervous at the altar. But we'd agree how amazing was the ring you'd brought her.

Then you'd have to go, but make sure you hold me first.

They were lucid dreams from a parallel multiverse.

You didn't meet your wife, but you're leaving both of us.

That's why I wake up at night and it feels like I'm choking up – I know that I was your first love, and you will be my last.

And every day I'm travelling closer to the stars, that's when we'll meet again, no need for telepathy and Mero's World will be our little legacy.

There is strength in reflection and courage in contemplation, especially in the face of adversity. When the past has left an indelible mark on the present, and the future is filled with a sense of emptiness, we can only hope to fill that void with daydreams and thoughts of love - wrap our sorrows in a blanket of warmth and channel our teardrops towards a place of growth. Face fears head on, go to war with our nightmares. Author Brene Brown says only when we are brave enough to explore the darkness will we discover the infinite power of our light. In writing about the loss of her beloved son, to a senseless and violent act in 2021, Kelly Brown does just that. Channelling her pain through her pen and immortalising her baby boy on the page. Creating a legacy that will live for as long as the stars. You are an inspiration to us all. Kelly, wear your heart on your sleeve, that's when they start to believe.

Eternally your friend and your advocate.

Written by Quinton Green, Youth Mentor

Where to find help

Mero's World Foundation
Kelly@merosworld.org.uk
www.meroworld.org.uk
Facebook: Merosworld West
Instagram: Merosworld2021
Twitter: Merosworld20211

Greater Manchester Violence Reduction Unit
Tootal/Broadhurst Building
56 Oxford Road
Manchester M1 6EU
Telephone Number: 0161 778 7000
GMVRU@greatermanchester-ca.gov.uk

1message.org.uk
Matthew Norford Chair of 1Message
1message@outlook.com
Facebook: 1message
Instagram: 1message2016
Twitter: 1message

Milton Keynes UK
Ingram Content Group UK Ltd.
UKHW020330031224
451863UK00012B/482

9 781917 425162